Happy Birt
to my l

THE GREAT BRITISH WRITE OFF

ACROSS ENGLAND

I was invited to provide
a poem for this book! page 244
hope you enjoy reading!
with love. Cynthia

Edited by Donna Samworth

forward**poetry**

First published in Great Britain in 2015 by:
Forward Poetry
Remus House
Coltsfoot Drive
Peterborough
PE2 9BF

Telephone: 01733 890099
Website: www.forwardpoetry.co.uk

Printed and bound in the UK by BookPrintingUK
Website: www.bookprintinguk.com

Foreword

Here at Forward Poetry our aim has always been to provide a bridge to publication for unknown poets and allow their work to reach a wider audience. We believe that poetry should not be exclusive or elitist but available to be accessed and appreciated by all.

Our latest competition 'The Great British Write Off' was created to celebrate the writing talent we have here in the UK. We invited poets and authors to write either a poem, a short story or even an extract from a novel that showcases their ability. The result is an entertaining collection of creative writing that expresses and communicates thoughts, feelings and ideas on a multitude of subjects. A panel of judges will now choose their top 4 authors, one each from England, Northern Ireland, Scotland and Wales. Each winner will win a prize bundle and the overall winner will receive a cash prize!

Whether you prefer humorous rhymes, poignant odes or a thrilling short story, there is something in these pages to suit every reader's taste. We are very proud to present this anthology and we are sure it will provide entertainment and inspiration for years to come.

Contents

The Creative Writing

Still Waters Run Deep

I was that quiet girl, who by the window sat,
The window that looked on the marshes flat,
A Mecca for wetland fowls of the air,
And elusive creatures, who filled ponds everywhere.

One foggy night at the unearthly hour,
I saw a heavenly meteorite shower,
Florescent stars burst all around,
Then magnetic rocks hurled to the ground.

The ponds had a strange force field,
And later new life, they did yield,
Creatures got bigger and bigger,
With bolder colours and lots of vigour.

With torch in hand, a searching I did go,
For an obscure energetic fellow,
Crawling through the reeds at night,
Wondering if I might get a fright.

Then jumping out of the water, from under a rock,
Was a huge amphibian, striped to shock,
Blowing bubbles galore, from mouth and rear end,
And croaking, 'I want you as a dear friend.'

I called him the nadderwater jack-ass toad,
Who often frequents my abode,
He sits on the ledge, young on his back,
Then returns to a pond, when it's dark as a sack.

Gillian Balsdon

The Lee Marshes

Once lush meadows spread to the water's edge
Of the meandering River Lee.
Once pure water flowed within.
And Charles Lamb walked its banks so green,
And for solace to its meadows once did go.
But that was a century or more ago.
Now black smoke billows from grey chimneys tall
Concrete factories have smothered all.
Whilst on the rest of vacant ground,
Rubbish tipped and domestic garbage
Scattered all around.
Amongst rusted tin cans, old cars discarded.
Brown and red empty hulks kissed by the wind.
Nature tries to conquer all and sparsely covers
Fertile patches with bracken weed and twitch grasses.
Then I saw him; a small boy dressed in blue.
Dirtied denim shirt of doubtful hue.
He was but six years of age.
In his hand he held a battered cage.
Once a shiny home for its bird owner proud.
Now just a twisted, corroded, rusty red.
He saw me not and in his imagination played.
On his finger perched an invisible bird.
To it he spoke and gathered food.
Only he could see its plumage coloured
With the sight only a child could know.
I saw him wave goodbye to his feathered friend,
As in his mercy he let it fly away.

Peter Coakly

The Suitcase

It's dark, it's cold, it's old
But it's mine
It's my suitcase
It's with me 24/7
Some say I need a new one but not that simple,
Not that easy, some days it's never opened,
Only when it's triggered,
Or maybe when I sit, think, reflect
And repeat the circle that's so transparent.
Those feelings are still among me, I try to escape it,
But the case gets heavier, I can feel the tension on my arm
As I hold but never let go.
The fate that comes and goes, I just keep getting wrong.
The list of fate forces it wide open,
The pressure, the anger builds up into one big emotion.
Then it won't shut, it stays open, leaving me staring down at the past.
I look down, I see you, I hear you, all those fallen promises, those mistakes.
You're still sat at the top of the suitcase, you're still there.
As if it was yesterday making me continue the never-ending story.
I just want to speak,
I want my voice to control it,
Make it shut, to make it close,
But instead I just echo your words which puts me in a forever test.
Some of the items are magnets that draw back into a solid memory freeze.
Where the confidence pours from within me.
The face becomes red, which makes me feel weak.
I look up and you're gone, making me long for more,
Which makes me dig deeper through all the dust,
All the cobwebs, removing all the unwanted items,
So that all the clear important stuff is laying at the top, undamaged.
Waiting for the circle to rediscover.

Sarah Cox

England

She danced along, with smile, no guile and laughter filled her days
The knaves, the swains, philanderers, with predatory gaze
Watched her with their hungry eyes and longing in their stare
But they mattered not to her, she simply did not care.

So out of reach, no sin within, and solitary ways
Hears the music of the free, which for her always plays
And if they offered lust or love or anything they dare
They could not hold her promise, for her shadow was not there.

He came her way, hair gold, so bold, with charm he'd break a heart
He'd hide a smile and shrug, so sad, when came the time to part
He played the game, oh Romeo, broke hearts collect on his sleeve
Just as he made them oh so sure, it was his time to leave.

Yet lied he not, no joke he spoke, seduction from the start
Lined up his shot, then aimed his bow, with most beguiling dart
Around a maid, his spell so well, thrice artfully he'd weave
But candid truth shines from his eyes, he's not one to deceive.

Then there she was, he saw so pure, her style, soft, sweet, demure
He felt strange stirrings in his soul, got lost in her allure
He kissed her palm, with feelings new and begged her, would she dance?
So and began, first time for each, desire to take love's chance.

Ardour bloomed, hearts sang, bells rang, love sick, but both were sure
Both struck down, honey sickness, for which there is no cure
His emerald eyes, they hypnotised and held her close, in trance
They lived, they loved, their passion swelled, with every silken glance.

The stars smiled down, red rose they chose, entwined their love forever
Not parted for one moment they, two halves, one whole together
But leopards do not change their spots, the oak and mistletoe
Survive along in greenwood, yet in pairing, well they grow.

But summers end, on call leaves fall and wither with the heather
And love runs cold and freezes in the bleak December weather
The feelings that had shook him and made his love reveal
Had quite dispelled and moving on was eager in appeal.

And so he left, no word she heard, she searched from dusk till dawn,
His whistle had gone from the woods, and how she wept, forlorn,
Grieved for her mate and sought him out, she knew not how to deal
With the sadness in her soul, where branded was his seal.

Then truth set in, she sighed then cried and swore on Christmas morn
Lived with a sadness, shattering, nigh too hard to be borne
For him, he never found a love, to pierce Achilles heel
For matchless she and peerless she had robbed his heart to feel.

Heidi Haversham

You Are My Tomorrow

Stood on the edge of a past unknown;
Solid black, dark without you, alone;
Ignorant to everything my world could be;
Ignorant of what your touch means to me;
Will I achieve my potential, or merely survive;
Will God be proud when I finally die?

Here and now, today, the present;
Feelings so new and yet so ancient;
You fill my world, my heart my soul;
So deep and entirely I won't be consoled;
Should our time be severed or come to an end;
I need you, my life, my love, my friend.

Stood on the verge of the rest of forever;
You're filling my world, the promised endeavour;
To use all my strength, to use all of my power;
Every God given moment, every last waking hour;
That the moment we marry and our hearts entwine;
Destiny will be written and life's meaning defined.

Where the stars shine brightest, looking back on my life;
My family, my friends, my children, my wife;
Souls destined to be, will follow each other;
Through time immemorial, one life to the other;
I smile with a warmth, shining bright deep inside me;
Safe in the knowledge my family will find me.

Stephen Smart

Lucas

By the silent loch
'neath stern fells
an old cottage sits
watching empty fishing boats
and factory farmed nets
through half-curtained eyes,
growing into the heather
and gorse that surround.

Enter the garden
past bustling beehives
and abandoned upturned dinghy,
pull wide the creaking door
past long unused servants' bell
down the darkened corridor.

To where the English boy
ate soup and then salmon
and made her smile
by asking for more.
In the long cupboard in
that kitchen.

Lies her gun,
covered by woollen blanket,
old, long handled musket
passed down father to son,
then due to necessity to daughter.

The elderly woman who
ladled the broth keeps
the heirloom clean and
the bullets safe and handy
ready to fight the English
should the need arrive.

In the dead of night
does she still sit
cradling the gun
while rocking patiently
hand straying from
knit to trigger
with apparent ease.

Andrew Scotson

Shades Of The Spectrum

Drowning in thoughts contradictory,
Won't you pull me out from under,
My vibrant girl of colour.

A sure shot with words,
Rage gracefully fired off with wisdom,
Already jaded with age,
My capricious girl of crimson.

Hard of mind not heavy of heart,
Logic shows you all the cracks,
Replace what you can't take back,
My bold girl in black.

We found each other in the grey,
Locked minds since then to defend one another,
Let's cocoon ourselves for the winter,
Then dance wildly in the summer,
Just you and I,
My violent girl of colour.

Dean Linsell

Persona

Gasping for a single solitary part of over generalisation
And it hits you through your obligatory mess and your unfunctional
organisation
You're alone in a world that spits upon your open ideas and revolutionary
dreams
Forever you are cast aside, years spent as a shadow for you it seems
Hollow victories come in dreaded moments, when it seems insane
But this life, as hard as it seems, this is always a game
Enjoyment comes when justifiably you force a smile on that mask you call a
face
Wearing that tattered and worn identity without a sense of grace
Succumb to people who crack the whip and order you around
They simply stand above you as they stamp your head into the ground
Jostling for something, maybe a glimmer of hope
That maybe one day you won't need those pills you call happiness,
Maybe one day you will cope.

Thomas Faulkner

Spares Or Repair

Jiggle, jiggle, wriggle and twist
You pull and tug with all your might -
To others in the room, you must look a sight
Your mouth contorted urgh -
The electrical pliers grabbing tight
To the tooth – that's putting up a terrific fight!
You keep mopping up the drool
An unwanted by-product from using this tool -
Nearly there . . .
Jiggle, jiggle, wriggle and twist
And 'voila' – you have in your hand
A one-inch member of the calcium factory
For spares or repair!

Bryan Montague

Little Red Flower

There's a little red flower grows where soldiers once stood
in the green fields of Flanders, it's the colour of blood.
This little red flower with petals unfurled
stands as a symbol of loss that's known through the world.
It stands for remembrance of those gone before
who gave up their lives in the midst of a war,
a symbol of pain, of loss and of sorrow
for those fallen heroes who gave us tomorrow.
So cometh the month and the day and the flower
remember the fallen and the little red flower.

Eric D. Bishop

This Is The Last Time

You are the echo in places after everyone's sound has gone.
You are the reluctant resonance in air between breaths.
You are the leaving that's overstayed its welcome.
You are the racket in deprivation of company.
You are the uproar after music has ceased.
You are the chord eternally reappearing.
You are reverberations of want, of lack.
You are sweet tinnitus in every hush.
You are every absent reoccurrence.
You are degradations of denial.
You are epitomes of entirety.
You, the unrelenting end.
Your gale still lingers.
But you do not.
You do not.
You do
not.

Ellie Gwen

Man (Dreaming)

He is the only other person on this bus.
His body is travelling west, but his mind is already nestled in the comfort of her chest.
He's the kind of man that's lived through his hands.
The kind of hands that are bulbous and creak from the bubbles of life stored between knuckles.
He puts roses on the seat next to him like he's cradling a newborn.
He's the kind of man who doesn't know what that feels like.
He's the kind of man that's never expected more than he's worth.
The kind of man that says the sea is just an overgrown lake and freedom of speech was a mistake.
The kind of man that wheezes after every comment he makes, but only to suck the breath back in in case someone takes it from him.
He fills his scars with tarmac because he was raised to believe that women avoid roads with potholes for fear of falling in them.
He's the kind of man who met a woman with the endurance to orbit his world.
But he met her ten years too late.
He built a thousand shelves and she became his thousand centrepieces.
He's the kind of man that only wears ties on nights like this.
The kind of tie that has been knotted with nervous fingers.
A tie that was once crimson and has faded to burnt umber.
A tie that droops from the collar to give his throat room, so he won't choke on his apology.
He's the kind of man who didn't know what do with a woman like her, so he pursued her like a tempest pursues the soil, but only to find she was a fully grown oak.
She was not there to be broken.
She is in his mind but I can see her, twisting her neck around his, spiralling like DNA.
She's the kind of woman with lips like bulldozers and legs like roots.
She rubs her eye shadow on like war paint and douses herself in that foggy musk of immortality.
She's the kind of woman that says everything is beautiful and everything is disgusting and she's spent her life figuring out where she should draw the line.
There was a time where the only lines she could bear were the ones she drew across her wrists.
She let him swim in her scars.
She's the kind of woman that has dolphin skin.

The kind of skin that ripples like sloe gin.
Skin thicker than the Berlin Wall she knocked down with a hair pin.
She met him at the right time and likes to remind him of the correct order of the pronouns.
She is an honest woman, who loves honest words from honest men.
She's the kind of woman that will accept his apology.
He presses stop.
He stands up, pats down his coat, picks up the roses, and gets off the bus.
I watch him cross the road. He stops for a moment to readjust his hat.
And that's when I see the church stained with ivy.
As the bus pulls away I see him walking towards a black gravestone.
I think of nothing else on my way home.

Charley Genever

Dear God

Dear God, you made a lovely place
'This world' a sphere that floats in space
with trees and flowers, forests grand
all coloured with an artist's hand.
Blue, green, the mighty oceans flow
like threads of ribbon through the globe,
a golden sun to give warmth and light
a silver moon to shine at night.
God, you made a Heaven – then did you ponder
and wonder what else you could do?
Were you fatigued with all that you had planned?
Did your hand falter, when you made Man?
Were you so tired, that you didn't see
what Man could do in his stupidity,
not foresee that Man could debase
the free will you gave to the human race,
that those who destroy with evil treachery
endanger this world, regardless of its beauty?
Dear God, could you not see what Man can do,
that you made amongst us, the good so few?

Josie White-Mackenzie

When You're Old

When you reach a certain age
I'll try not to be coy.
The over eighties say
That's life's not full of joy.

It could be really nice to do
The things you used to do
Your legs are stiff, your shoulders ache
Your eyes are dimmer too.

You look into the mirror
The real you isn't there.
The wrinkles are so obvious
And you're not supposed to care.

You may have lost the love of your life
You try not to let it show,
But now and then it does still hurt,
Nobody really knows.

But then your children come to call
They are so good to you.
And then your grandchildren come as well
How special they are too.

You have such wonderful memories
When you were young long ago
Of the loving parents that you had
And how you loved them so.

Your brother used to tease you
He'd sometimes make you mad
But the love you shared with him
You feel so lucky that you had.

So when you're feeling low
And feeling old and sad,
Think of all the riches in your life
And all the love that you have had.

Love is all that matters
Whether you're young or old
When you feel that you are loved
That love is worth more than gold.

Love comes from within
It doesn't get wrinkled or old.
It shines through everything you do
If you let it – when you're old!

Vera Seddon

A Night At The Opera

Here we are at the opera,
Isn't it a treat?
Although we're up in the gallery,
These are decent seats.

Have you brought the glasses;
To give us a closer look,
And did you study the libretto;
That little opera book?

If you want to follow the story,
That's the thing to do.
Otherwise it can be tricky
If you haven't got a clue!

Being performed in Italian,
Is really rather good;
Albeit sung in English,
More easily understood?

But hush, the lights are dimming,
The conductor has come in;
The curtains now are parting
And the opera is about to begin!

Peter Mahoney

Balsall Heath

The store across the road bristles with the multicultural community,
Casually, choosing vegetables;
Tomatoes, okra, aubergines and chillies;
Looking furtive.
Some in burkhas, some with sandals, some with shalwa cemises
The shop assistant stands here, talking,
Singling out change for a purchaser.

The maisonettes stretch way down Hallam Street.
Up the road Victorian houses, with gardens;
Full of chattering and screaming children,
Playing all evening,
Unashamedly noisy,
And their cries reach my ears, inside my flat.

The Sikh temple lies also nearby.
Sometimes they have big weddings there.
Once there was a marquee up between us and them.
Hordes of them gathered, thronging the parking spaces.
I saw the bride and groom, once.
Cars queue down the road.
Children and adults, cascading out of the windows,
Calling gaily to each other;
Their swarthy-skinned faces, lit up;
Drums, rumbling in the distance.

Occasionally, there's a big cricket match at the stadium,
The barrage of cheering and talking.
A hubbub of clatter.
If you're out walking, it hits you.
The ground is massive,
Like a huge flying saucer with windows.
From time to time, it exudes crowds of spectators.
It rivals Cannon Hill Park.

The park has its beds of bright tulips;
Its rhododendrons,
a colourful jostle;
with tree-lined walks;
its little café for elevenses,
for sustenance;
the ponds with ducks and and occasional long-beaked heron;

the once-new MAC, and its exhibitions;
ready to beguile,
in its upstairs studio,
its other expensive café,
where a coffee is nearly two pounds.
I sit there sometimes, partaking,
at a table, having waited in a queue
in the gallery, the guides are pleasant and accommodating.

Outside the River Rea sends its gushing water over small cataracts and its bridges
hold spectators and plodders, some observing.
In the park, there's crazy golf,
and a life-like statue of a golfer,
looking very real.
And the busy car park, and its metal gyrations of chrome

Round the corner,
on Salisbury Road Hill
horse chestnuts tower upwards,
resplendent,
above the busy grind of traffic

And Amberly Court nursing home lies there silently,
concealing bedridden invalids and recluses,
its sensory garden lies there,
packed in by trees.

Judy Fleetwood-Walker

Fire

I find you hard to analyse
For my description puts you down
Almost as something to despise.

Then I think again, for somewhere is something fine you do
Burning in the imagination, living in the heart and soul
Of those who would create, powering them ever onward
To reach the ultimate.

You draw me closer in wintertime
Controlled and generating heat, to warm my feet
One face of you dispenses charm, the other harm.

Horrific are your ways if left alone unguarded
No limit to the sadness which you bring
Like pestilence, plague, and flood
You have become an evil thing.

I do look for the best in you
And it is true, your flame is carried high for liberty
And smaller flames are lit in praise of he
Who died to set us free
It's plain to see your power demands we keep you in captivity.

You touch me too, and urge me ever on to bigger, better things
When all is done, it's strange to think we two became as one
Just heaps of ash, blown on by the wind, and gone.

Edith M Wooldridge

St Francis Of Assisi

'Where is he now, that Franciscan Friar
Who worshipped even the mouse?'
He's sitting by his heavenly fire,
Stacking coins in his counting house.

The polished planks of his plush wooden floors
Were stolen from old Noah's Ark.
He massages them with the bees' wax he hoards
And buffs them with a skylark.

He rolls on his lush rug of tiger skin
And his comforting goose eiderdown.
He does not see his stuffed bear as a sin,
He admires it in his ermine gown.

He surrounds himself with bright butterflies
For their value is so dear to him.
He sees his collection as tasteful and wise,
Glass-framed with smooth snakeskin trim.

His favourite meal is stewed veal and honey
Followed by quail in red wine.
He turns and counts his heaps of bribe money
When prayers ask of Earth's creatures' decline.

He scratches the backs of conglomerates
And his own with an ivory rod.
He hides his house with palm fronds
When he senses he's being watched by God.

James Heaney

The Vaunt

The air is warm tonight upon the hills,
These earthy, old, grass-gilded hills of home.
Restless in breezing murmur, time is hushed
And I, in sacred sanctuary – not rushed -
Inherit all this rolling heather sea
That's scratched by yellow gorse and budding ling.

How quietly the day draws to its close
The trodden path, frequented much, retires;
The sky unfurls its wild diurnal fire.
Matchless in colour, vivid beauty shows
So strong in strains of amber, red and gold,
But quickly wanes to violet most desired.

And then in dusking silence comes her trill
And nothing might dislodge her in this calm:
The comfort notes of song from Heaven's sill
Tumble and turn and vault in breathless rills
And surge, clamouring to sound brave alarm
And hold this place forever out of harm.

John Blackmore

The Rainbow – Pope Benedict XVI At Auschwitz

Herded by murderers, they went this way.
Line after line they passed; day after day.

A man walks through the rain. He's come to pray.

It's lonely in the cold grey shadows there.
Evil seems lingering in the lifeless air
And the great world sunk deep into despair.

Man born for love is turning from love's light,
Blind to that beauty fairer than the height
Where the stars are, blaze, flaming silver-white.

The wall of death towers desolate and bare.
Is God himself no longer anywhere?

Yet still the man is standing there, in prayer.

And now when noon of day seems dark as night,
A rainbow shines with colours made so bright
Only God, who is love, could bring this light.

Diana Momber

Oh, England

The rolling, sweeping fields of light gold
Reveal freshly-tilled lands of summer wealth,
Worked by ardent farmers from days of old,
Men of the soil bring forth a promising health -
And feed the poor, the rich and those oppressed,
Who, from their labours, seek their rest.

A lone tree, in a green field, guardian of all,
Golden acres awaiting the farm-hands,
Sheltering, granting their need of bread, cheese and ale
For many years past, keepers of these lands -
A proud hornbeam, surveying her earth,
Stately and tall in this isle of her birth.

Oh, the stories she could tell, had she a voice
Of the promises made, some kept, some broken,
Beneath her outspread branches, made a choice -
Many a maid wearing treasured love-tokens,
And our old tree, her secrets forever her own,
As she battled all the elements, thriving so alone.

Bright red poppies amongst bales of hay,
Where hares and little field-mice at eventide appear
And owls swoop over, where bats hold sway,
The farmer and his dog strolling by, are near -
To a welcoming log; beneath the trees' bowers to rest
And survey the English scene, both feel blessed!

A place of peace – their own haven sought,
Reflecting on all that the day had brought,
Beneath her ample shade – in that leafy glade.

Julia Eva Yeardye

Love In Life After Death

I will give you my heart as I take my last breath
Because our love will live on in life after death,
My heart may stop, my love for you will not
In Heaven, as on Earth you're never forgot.

I want my last words to be 'I love you'
And the last that I hear . . . 'I love you too.'
I want your eyes to be the last sight I see
Before the skies of Heaven light up for me.

And on Heaven's staircase, for you I will wait
To see the smile on your face at Heaven's gate,
Because it makes my heart race and pupils dilate
With irreplaceable feelings that you create.

So, for the touch of your hand my hand waits
As I stand on the steps by the pearly gates,
Waiting every day for you to arrive
So the love we shared we can revive.

And as I patiently wait in anticipation
I sit and reflect in contemplation,
Recollect and compile a compilation
Of every smile that was your creation.

And when the skies above Earth turn grey in dismay
Candles will burn bright on Heaven's stairway,
As we reunite the hearts we'll never betray
And reignite the love that never went away.

For the second time, it's love at first sight
As you steal my heart and Heaven's limelight,
And as I carry you over Heaven's threshold
The flames of passion make Hell seem so cold.

Stuart Brisco

A Lament For Home

I long for you,
Yearn for you,
My heart burns for you,
I just hate leaving you each painful time.
A home for always in a heart needing love,
A vessel, glass-like, to shatter in a beat,
When life keeps me far, when I can't be near.

You speak to me clear in your streets, filled with folk,
A true melting pot of flotsam and jetsam,
from corner far flung, from their sacred home.
A dream to fulfil?
A journey long?
Has brought them to you,
As I leave your arms.

A blue running vein of power,
Keeps calling me home,
And brings me great strength,
It ebbs and it flows, it takes and it gives.
A life blood of hope,
For times that are good and times that are bad,
A start or an end, a pool full of tears,
For those gone away, or those lost here.

I don't want to leave the place I call home,
To journey away till next I come near.
To refresh, recharge, to make me anew
By just being home and near to you.
I long for your grip, your gentle caress,
Your feminine touch which holds me right here.

A place filled with hopes a place filled with dreams
It's all up to you, we'll carry you there,
To stardom or fame
Or day-to-day grind
We're rooting for you to make your breakthrough.
Be you pauper or prince we'll treat you the same
With dignity and love for you being you.

A place filled with old a place for the new,
A history long, with long future too.

A castle for kings, a people's great hall,
Monuments a few, a Cavern Club too.
A city of play, of industry too
A place of hard work, learning, findings anew.

A place to call home, a place to lay roots,
No matter how far a soul they may roam.
I long for your touch, to be in your streets
To lay in your parks, and bask in your glow.
A place that's all mine, a place that's yours too
A place I hold dear, a home for all time,
The city of two halves, the city that is one,
The city of open arms, my Liverpool home.

Simon Peter Bartley

The Voice

I opt for silence. You shout.
This does not mean I do not speak.
Your voice is far louder than mine;
Does that mean mine should not be heard?

I am strong within; you are strong without
This does not mean that I am weak.
Dismissal without your giving me time,
Seems to me a little absurd.

I choose to trust; you choose to doubt
This does not mean my cause is bleak.
Though we be not the same in mind
If we divide, then we have erred

Though my countenance be still without
Still water does run deep.
Future forward, past behind
May that line ne'er be blurred.

Simon Day

For David

The first time we met, I could see,
That you and I were meant to be,
Your touch so gentle, your smile so true,
Your hair so wispy, your eyes so blue.

I think of you as I stir in the morning,
Knowing it's for you that I have fallen,
I dream of you throughout the night,
You are my soulmate, my fella, my knight.

You make me feel like I'm a queen,
Like being inside an amazing dream,
Our love is real, of that I know,
And each day that love will always grow.

A bond so strong, a hold so tight,
To know you're the one, my Mr Right,
You seem to fit just like a glove,
In you I've found my one true love.

I can't express the love I feel,
Waiting for the day when you will kneel,
You are my hero, my baby, my Dave,
You've swept me away just like a wave.

I know in my heart that you're the one,
Through everything you've said and done,
And now for the rest of our lives to start,
To us, our future – You've stolen my heart.

Tara Traverse

His Real Angel

He called her his angel,
She's in his dreams,
Now she's an angel,
She visits him in his dreams.

He didn't want to leave her,
Nor say goodbye,
But he had to leave her,
And let her die.

He's broken-hearted,
Since she went away,
And since they departed,
He wanted her to stay.

Till the very end,
He always used to say,
She was his best friend,
He loved her each day.

She always cried,
And he'd wipe her tears,
She wanted to die,
She hid her fears.

She left him for good,
She'll never come back,
He cries in her hood,
She's not coming back.

Kirstymarie Hill

Attempting Poetry

Voices in my ear, taking shape,
The marble of language to new design,
On the eye of the soul new visions drape
Themselves, a skeleton of sounds refine.
Smooth white hopefulness, I chisel in trust,
A monument, whatever it shall be
I know not yet, to hurry is unjust,
Though its bright young future I yearn to see.
Singing the universe into a rhyme,
Or trying that at least, croaking my hymn,
To the music playing through me this time,
Before my inspiration shall grow dim.
Flying above dull silence like a bird,
New worlds can be spoken in sacred word.

Christopher Villiers

Always Blue

Now you have died
Life's not the same way
Blue always turns to grey.
Whatever I do
I think of you
Whatever I say
Your presence is here every day.
It brightens my life
With thoughts of you
But then it goes from blue to grey
And I think about when you were taken away.
My life is now
Blue, grey and black
I know you are never coming back
I cannot cope with losing you
So my days may be always blue.

Trudie Sullivan

Survivor

Shocked into an immovable statue by the cold wind,
Chilled to the very marrow I stand as if frozen in time,
My desperate attempts to intake as little air as allows for life to continue,
Each breath like swallowing icy sharp needles of pain
that stab and twist from lips to lungs,
Each small slow exhale only proving that there is life still beneath the
many layers of cloth that hides so well our fragility to the icy cough
of nature that now punches and tears at my frailty, stealing more
and more breath with each jab and swing of its mighty fist,
The desire to survive ebbing away,
The rhythmic beat of life growing slower, fainter,
A tiredness sweeping over me,
I command my legs to move but they disobey . . . not today,
Yet I must persevere, carry on, not give in, not give up,
Determined I tell myself I will see tomorrow, I will go on,
Fight this fear, ignore this pain, I must go on,
Forever onward, forever forward, never ceasing, never easing, never stopping,
For to stop is to drop and to drop means death and death shall not have me,
Not today, it's not my time,
Not while there is still some small pittance of strength left somewhere within
my being,
Yet if by chance I do fail and death be the victor,
The tale shall tell that I fought tooth and nail, dug as deep as
I could and fought the hardest of fights,
I didn't flicker out softly, silently like a candle in the wind,
I roared like a lion, clawing and biting until the last
breath left my worn-out exhausted body,
Yet that time is not yet upon me and may never well be and to dwell upon
such negativity is one step closer to the end and I?
I am only at the beginning,
I am not yet ready to leave this world that I love and all the wonders it holds,
I will survive,
I will grow old.

John McGee

Skopija

Hookah pipe puffing, silver flashing cut-throat razors
dancing around the swarthy faces of the narrow-eyed
Arab liquorice moustached pubic curl
Sat icy frozen still in the blistering daylight
not to spill a sneezing spot of rose red nectar from their faces
the razor a silver fish on a yellow sea

Every clothing, cloth, radio part and mouldy moth
strewn and displayed for sale at any price
Tobacco shoe boxed tanned dry trimmings
aromatic magic tricks to tempt the eyes
Back street time, stop watched, stopped clock
history repeating never moving test of time

Chiming wailing minarets stab Christian clouds to death
bleeding Islamic blue tiled rain cracking on the skull-capped wonderers
Moorish tourists

Rambling cobbles snake and slither through the smells
of lamb and musk and incense and insanity
bulging eyes roll over laughing bellies
of the linened fat cat tea drinking
business in the blink of a foreign eye

Mutton fat sticky windows
sheep dipping dripping bread
chilli hot steaming shops
of crystal clean surgical spirited sterile tables
munching down nose running vinegar stroked
eye-watering taste buds swirling around dervishly

Pitki stacked as laundry white dusted flour flat breads
as unrisen as a teenager on a school morning lazy, yeastless and full of wind

Time forgotten history book pages
still photographs of an age still living
breathing in the dust of time's ticking clock
Long gone bubbling bloodstained streets

congealed in the cracks sparrow pecking
hack puh sunflower seed spitting tuberculosis
black death, creeping death watch beetle
tick-tock, tick-tock.

James Morgan

Such Sweet Memories . . .

A hint of summer longing sung in sweet tones,
Gentle earthy scents crept the tips of our nose.
As gorse and broom brushed fields mellow,
Well-dressed trunks now spread the wintered gaps in tumbling hedgerows.
Oh such sweet memories . . .
The chamomile hills rolled away,
Swooping swifts to the seas.
Sewn in the wild hedge rose,
Neatly brewing shades of leaves.
Where tapestry reaches every well earthed place,
Upon a ridge, to for a while just sit and gaze.
Oh such sweet memories . . .
Perfumed orchids tempted fox trots,
Serene courting, painted ladies hopped in bug love,
Humming along with the bumbling bees,
Barley grass weaving the breeze.
Oh such sweet memories . . .
Greened wheat laden autumn promises kissed the land,
Riding gallant as hare and hand.
Foot falls rhythm echoes naturally,
Rambling along a warm yellow vista beautifully.
The call of the wilds rugged simplicity,
So deeply embraced with nature's melody.
Oh such sweet memories . . .
Such sweet memories.

Natasha Georgina Barrell

29

Apache (Trail Of Tears)

He stands tall upon the valley ridge
Sees the sunset's orange glow
He looks down upon the trail of tears
To where his nation died below
He remembers how they used to live
Their teepees on the plains
How they'd hunt the wild buffalo
Those days will never be again

He rides a snow-white stallion
That takes him everywhere
He remembers all his ancestors
And the territories they all shared
The river valleys verdant green
High places where the air is clean
And crystal streams where he once would dream
What happened to those days?

The white man came and stole his land
Drove his tribe onto desert sand
His braves resisted bows in hand
But the white man had his way
Settlers staked their stolen lands
Red blood spilled on desert sands
And where the Winchester was brought to play
His braves died every day.

He remembers how things used to be
Wild honey from the honeybee
Songs around the campfires
And blossoms in the trees
Each tribe respected others' lands
Seldom things got out of hand
They lived in peace the Indian bands
Until the trail of tears.

The wild buffalo made few demands
Roaming 'cross their sacred lands
They were never killed for pleasure
Or for greed
The buffalo are all but gone
Now cattle herds ten thousand strong

Pollute the streams and rivers
And desecrate the land.

He wonders why it had to be
The red man lived in harmony
He had known the land and sunk its song
For generations long
But he was driven from the place he knew
Such hatred for the chosen few
Did all the killing all the dying
Justify the greed?

The crystal streams no longer flow
Though the valley still sits far below
But the river now is dammed
And overflowing
Barbed wire fences line the ground
Tractors roar where there was once no sound
And as the Apache Indian chief stands looking down
His tears fall to the ground!

He rode a snow-white stallion
That took him everywhere
Now he's with his long lost ancestors
In the territories they share
He stands tall upon the valley ridge
Sees the sunset's orange glow
Looking down upon the trail of tears
Where his nation died below!

David K Wilson

Mole Of The Universe

Two moles came up for air,
In the middle of a well kept green.
They gazed up at the starry sky,
And marvelled at the scene.

'So let me get this straight.'
The younger mole began.
'You're telling me it's infinite,
But there isn't any plan?'

'Well sort of,' said the older mole,
'We know it follows certain rules,
But we think they're not deliberate,
Because creationists are fools.'

'So, one day there was nothing,
And then there was a bang,
And after that there's stars and stuff,
And that's how it all began?'

'That's right, I think,' the old mole said,
Then blinked and rubbed his eyes.
It really was quite baffling,
To contemplate its size.

'So, if not by design,
Why then is it here?
Can an unthinking process,
Not be a puppeteer?'

'Consider this,' the old mole said,
'The matter of intent is mute,
If there were a great creator,
Its motive would be in dispute.'

This gave the young mole pause for thought,
Why would you make a thing like this?
If you can make a universe,
What need have you for deer and fish?

'Who would not,
If they could make,
A wondrous thing,
For wonder's sake?'

The old mole smiled and said, 'OK,
I'm glad to see you think,
But beware of where you're going
Lest to the depths you sink.'

'For if all the worlds are folly
Then this one must be too,
And all who live within them,
Including me and you.'

This did the young mole flummox,
He'd never thought his life was just,
An aesthete's passing fancy,
Or a random sequence of stardust.

Seeing life can have no meaning,
He turned and dug back in his hole,
And went to hunt some worms to eat,
As for all that, he was still a mole.

David Smith

World War One

A war to end all wars, they said,
How could that possibly be?
All those men, all dead and gone,
A loss to humanity.

You cannot imagine what it was like,
Out in those trenches there,
With bombs and firing all around,
Would anyone start to care?

Do not forget those who went,
Nor those who gave their all,
For freedom, love, and democracy,
They helped us after all.

Remember them on November 11th,
At 11 o'clock am,
A war to end all wars they said,
Let's never do it again.

Kath Lee

She

She is the star in my everlasting night
an immortal divinity to call my own
the only love
She is my narcotic; an addiction
deep in the roots of my being

We've had days of kisses, gentle and promising;
a beautiful pledge of the future to come
an eternal hope
We've had days of fighting, hopeless arguments
filled with desperate frustration

I've spent nights in awe of her beauty
tracing delicate patterns on delicate skin
intoxicated with passion
I've spent nights alone, with only my thoughts of her
a ceaseless torture of my wildest dreams

There are times she makes me laugh,
endless laughter spilling from my lips
easy happiness
There are times she makes me cry,
bittersweet tears of agonising love that burns and aches

There are simple days; days of sweet togetherness
untouched by the outside world; she captures
every waking moment
There are exhilarating days; days of dangerous enthralment
when I am lost in the entirety of her

Some nights she feels like stardust,
Enticing my senses and awakening my wonder
a true enchantress
Other nights she feels like mercury in my veins,
poisoning my every desire

She is the saviour of my suffering heart,
breathing her spirit into me; she creates
an exquisite existence
She is the sin invading every idea, belief, every fantasy
until I am consumed by her

34

She is the reason time stands still
the soft caress of a thousand nights,
an alluring seductress
She is an intense journey of sensuality and adoration,
enrapturing all with the electricity she leaves behind

And she is mine.

Tara Wells-McCulloch

Father Time

Father Time went round the rows of houses
with the crows and the cats and his stooping shoulders
one of the first of the early morning men
one of the last of a kind of a time back then.

On seasoned routes went his old boots – on his treadmill -
in laps and loops; an old boy unable to keep still.
With rules and routines ringing in his bones,
he threaded his way over cobblestones.

Like a needle, tending his patch of the North;
steady as stitch, going back and forth.
Like a pilgrim – just an old timer, him and the sun
in all weathers, just keeping his nose in front.

Half a century of housing has blocked out the view
around the mills, sandblasted back good as new
taking over that moorland of curving beauty
still, the bonds of time; the sense of duty.

One timeless day the streets were quiet as a shell;
time had stopped, so I heard the neighbours tell.
So I sang a song to mark the spot;
plant a sapling where he stooped to a stop

where the last grains of him dispersed
like salt unto the Earth.

Daniel Greenwood

Serendipity

Serendipity! The collective eclectic soul.
'That's me!'
The sun, it shines and gives to me
The chiaroscuro that I see.
The moon that glimmers in the night
That throws its spectre on the world,
A world of sun and rain and wind and ice
And snow. And I can gather all I see
And create a world of wonder just for me.
I paint my world and bring it here to me.
Serendipity!
Pebbles in streams, birds in trees,
Ponies in fields, clouds in the sky,
Secondhand clothes at sales
I can change into pieces of magic art
and use my skill and create my wardrobe.
And all because of serendipity.
It's in my soul, my art, my work, my poetry.
And it is completely free.
Whilst immersed in my world of books
I discovered 'serendipity'.
Serendipity, a word not old, not new,
But it describes my life, my soul.
It's good to know it's part of me.
And all my life I now can see
Has been a life of serendipity.
Discovery!
Boredom's not a thing I know,
Because the magic of life
Is always there in front of me.
I know there's those who do not praise me
When I say, 'What a wonderful world!'
Of course there's pain, there's misery.
I've known it all and yet I clearly see
That because of serendipity I do not fall,

Well not for long. It keeps me strong.
It embellishes my thinking, opens my eyes,
My mind and moves my fingers.
And that's the magic world of serendipity.

Joan Elizabeth

Can't Protect Her

I cannot give her what she needs
Can't offer her protection
I cannot end her crippling fear
Of heartache and rejection

I can't free her from her demons
Can't cure her mental health
She is her own worst enemy
I can't save her from herself

I cannot change the way she feels
Can't watch her 24/7
I cannot stop her biggest wish
To be an angel in Heaven

I can't keep her out of danger
Or safe away from harm
I cannot take away the pain
That's etched upon her arm

I cannot wave a magic wand
To vanish all her scars
I can't prevent her trying to achieve
Her dream to be in the stars

I cannot rescue my dearest friend
From the depths of her despair
I cannot make her any better
All I can do is be there.

Jade Bradley-Melling

Where Were His Slippers?

Slumped in the chair
In a melancholic nightmare
At a loss to where he put his slippers
Sitting there for days, or so it seems
Alternating between fear and
His once lived for dreams
Of twirling her around once again
Holding her in his tender embrace
Heartbeats mimicking each other
His love enveloping her
in those heady days of grace.

He'd been lucky, he'd been blessed
60 years of loved-up-ness
Yes, they quarrelled
With plenty of disagreements
But never forgetting the acorn
of love that brought them together
growing into the oak tree
of soulful agreement.

Once again
Wondering where he put his slippers
Once again
On the grieving big dippers

But then something clicked
As though the sadness circuit tripped
Then he heard her whisper, 'Darling,
Your slippers, they're on your feet'
Looking down in tears, there they were
'No time to waste, live now,' she said
'We've got more years to again meet.'

From that day forward, he always
Knew where his slippers were
No longer moving through life in a blur
Taking comfort in their eternal love
Time was a healer, that was for sure.

Jacqueline White

38

Wedded Bliss . . .

The wedding day came with wind and rain,
It tugged at our hats as we walked down the lane,
Into the church we sat on a pew,
Right at the front, what a good view,
The groom stood by with his mum,
Holding a hip flask full of rum,
Quietly we waited for the bride,
To walk up the aisle and stand alongside,
The vicar then married them double quick,
No time to pull out that's the trick,
They both said 'I do' with a bit of a grin,
To love one another through thick and thin,
A hymn was sung we knew it by heart,
Everyone stood up glad to take part,
The service was over it ended with a kiss,
Happy together in wedded bliss,
We threw confetti into the air,
And quietly said a silent prayer,
Off to the reception for a champagne toast,
A piece of salmon and an excellent roast,
The cake stood high in all its glory,
The making of which is another story,
The best man's speech was rather a hoot,
And in places quite astute,
The bride and groom had the first dance,
Beautiful together a true romance,
The disco started with flashing lights,
Women dancing, hitching up their tights,
Men throwing shapes on the dance floor,
You know the next day they're gonna be sore,
Much drinking was done throughout the night,
The tales of which I shall not write,
The day was done it ended well,
We waved them off with a fond farewell,
Together forever, married at last,
Thanks for inviting us, it's been a blast!

Cherry Cobb

Bussed

Liquorice light licked a lane
Hand picked again, gander graciously
Ferocious yet playfully pleasing
Teasing a berserk tear jerk
For mechanical monkeys
Roll up
  Roll up
      Slender sleeves
Pampered paper ludicrously leaves
Snuck in a Sunday sneeze a breeze
  So pleased to
Impress in an infected chest finesse
And the fickle flake barely awake
In a deep fried injunction of an
Institutional luncheon spared
For the lolly gaggers
  Narcissistic naggers
    Stranger stragglers
      And
Faceless hagglers hindering on a
Hearsay saved for some
Trudging tiresome tinsel town
And the wheels of the bus
Go round and round . . .
  To the hustle, bustle of a
Rambunctious rustle or rustic
Repeats
      Sodden seats the cheap
But sweet blare of the bleak
Tweaking tyrannosaurs twisting
  Mr and Missing
Carnivorous kissing
Now hissing in a horrendously heckled
Horror show, chauvinistic ballistic
Go nowhere's staring in each other's
Mother and lovers laced in a minestrone
Matrimony mayhem,
      But no one is ever sorry for
      Them
The sight of their plight

A slight slander quietly
Blander in an uphill meander
Menacing in itchy feet
  Ungraciously given up gangway
  Seats and windows down
And the wheels of the bus go round and
Round . . .
     The steep steps of the 22 the
Argumentative armpit of a kanga ruse
To name a few of this and that
  Tat splat, matt beard, pretty posture
Pretty weird posing, supposing
Juxtaposing in juvenile jurisdiction
A conman's contradictory can-can span
A plan for the sporadically intergalactic
Tracked in a tarmac caress, he really
Cared for you to see him
Care
   Less for the bitter bite of
Late night respites normally now sat
Informally inflated in belated clobber
Slobber, slipping shopper
Point to point harvested in a hectic
Heat and here comes
     Here comes
     Here comes
The steep step down
  And the wheels of the bus go round
  And round . . .
      Sit down!
An order to sit by the driver
An order to sit by the skiver
An order to sit by the jiver, striver, potential reviver for a fiver
Pocket rustle, corduroy shuffle
Wax jack tussle and he bites the bit
And he knows that they know that
It smells like it
But he's bold, but he's brash
Canny count out cash
And at last the
     Pacemaker set to

Stun
He'd never ever, ever, ever, ever felt so
  Young
Sung in brittle breezes, silent sighs
Of how and whys has it come
To this
      Bordering breakdown from bothersome
      Boys, that's not music that's
      Not even noise, treacherous tyranny
      From troublesome teens
          And
Turn that terribly ripe tripe
Down
And the wheels of the bus go round and
  Round . . .

Ross Bryant

Are We Alone?

This is the time
This is the place
Meet the universe
Face to face

And ask it how
It got so far
And what exactly
Is a star

And how the Earth
Has come to be
A solo world
Infinitely

Countless planets
Gleam in space
Yet are we alone
The human race.

Robert Stevens

The Girl

It wasn't the walk through the wood that made me catch my breath, it was seeing the girl. She was leaning against the gate, which separated the path from the beach. Her profile was very lovely, her skin albino white, her gaze unseeing. The setting sun created a halo effect around her pale, long, wavy hair. The whole picture was uncanny – ethereal like the image of Marianne, Pattie or Stevie, those icons of the past. One hand rested lightly on the rough wooden gate post while the other clutched the flimsy shawl, which could give her no real warmth. She was dressed all in white, some sort of muslin fabric, and her feet were bare. She must have felt the chill of the sea breeze but while I shivered, she remained still. I was near enough now to hear her breathing, but I heard nothing except the roar of the sea. She showed no awareness of anyone being so close to her, of anyone wanting to pass her. I reached out to touch her arm but felt only the damp stickiness of the cobweb on top of the gate. She was gone, leaving behind the taste and smell of sea salt tinged with the perfume of parma violets and a feather soft kiss on my cheek. The image, caught in a few moments of time, became framed in my memory like the Sarah Moon photos on my bedroom wall.

Mary Chapman

Beyond The Door

There is a door closed fast with growth that seals it tight,
As consequences of the past keep everything from the light.
And wanting to release the door the gardener, patiently
Waits the time when he will see the door swinging free.
He knows however long it takes the work there is to do
The growth must go, allowing him to enter and pass through!

And so it is with Man, whose heart is under sway
Of worldly growth that chokes, preventing freedom's way.
Bound by consequences of the past he needs to use
The handle on the inner side, whose heart can thus refuse?
For joy awaits beyond the door that holds the key
To life anew. Blessings sure and happiness for all eternity!

Beyond the door the answer lies what life is meant to be,
And is not found until the day the door is swinging free!

Elizabeth Bruce

There Was An Old Woman

Who sat at her desk
She had so many emails
She didn't know what to do!

Can't file them in the bin
That would be a sin
File them in the system
That would be quite grim
Too much about my waistline
And how to keep it slim
Too much about the bargains
That I'm about to win
If only I could only zap them
It would be a relief
But that involves three stages
And I am earning wages
I wish that I could have a wand
Or throw the emails in the pond
Alas I do not have one
So I must plot and plod
The emails grow like topsy
Like weeds that are all flopsy
I must be strong
I must take hold
Before the system
All runs cold
Then I could just sit and dream
And let my life begin.

Barbara Tozer

Nottingham – My City

It began its life in the caves by the River Trent
The first village on the site was known as Snottingham
Built by the Snots who lived in the locality
Nottingham blossomed into a wonderful city.

A place renowned for its commerce and industry
Whose famous sons have become part of our history
Its many qualities have been unfurled
Making it well known around the world.

The textile and cycle manufacturing are no more
These businesses have been exported to a foreign shore
Nottingham was renowned for the quality of its lace
Unfortunately other materials have come to take its place.

The names of John Player and Jesse Boot are easily identified
Their place in our history cannot be denied
And the effect of the legend of Robin Hood
Is something which is easily understood.

Nottingham is a wonderful place to visit
Its entertainments are numerous and beyond compare
With cricket, football, tennis, rugby and ice hockey
And many activities in the redesigned Market Square.

So much about Nottingham has been written on history's page
We are fighting to protect our heritage
It's a place which means so much to me
I am proud to live in a city with so much history.

Ronald Martin

Furious Love

The age-old story, another manifestation,
a different generation, same masquerade.
Eyes wide open, knowledge received,
freed from deception, I can finally breathe.
My weakness exposed, nowhere to hide,
my shameful secret I still despise.
Awakened beginning, a voice out of the dark,
hesitant juvenile, a nervous heart.
Reluctant servant, questioning trust,
double-minded obedience, shameful lust.
Fragile faith, confidence crushed yet
answers found, priority sorted, peace at last.

Deviating digression, stray from the path,
the trail is narrow, the earth is rough.
Focus adjusted, progression marred,
contorting in agony, spiritual scars.
Absurdist humour, refuse be human,
we're not better than this world, to the rules we're not immune.
Inspiring lies, substanceless hollow,
warm-worded fleetings, no foundation of stone.
An outlet of anger, no rules constricting,
frustrating laws, spine trembling.
Always questioning, the coward's clutch,
a vain exploration, a kiss too much.

Undeserved wail, collapse by the sea,
emptiness growing, experimenting.
Heaviness raining, a sombre house beat,
a four-to-the-floor soliloquy.
No rest for the boy, fear in his eyes,
stalked at every corner, demonised.
A consciousness trap, traumatic initiation,
flattery: a backhanded sincere imitation.
Faithless saint, stunned, forsook;
searching for God, refusing his book.
Twisted mind, fractured view,
if you tread that road, woe upon you.

I know what lurks in the recesses of thought,
vice-filled pursuits, pits for strays to be caught.

I wish I could be grateful, but the pride of the living
and acts of the flesh tear me from within.
Reduced to writing, expression neutralised,
relationships deserted, love digitised.
I don't know what I want, stop pretending;
the faintest spark of myself, flame unending.
A plane of glass, weight unbearing,
the cracks grow deeper, sound penetrating.
Injured but not fallen, an incomplete kill,
a sorry half-life, a tortuous thrill.

Symbols and lines, decipher the truth,
calligraphic forms requiring proof.
Unchained inside, outside a slave,
a logic sect, attempt at being brave.
A pointless exercise in light of God's Son,
answers in numbers, Genesis One.
Drowning in my sin, an excuse of an adult;
where's your initiative, walking algorithm?
A rock and a hard place, toil unfulfilling,
agendas incompatible, caught in-between.
'Intelligence' – I don't need it to survive,
an 'education' – what a waste of time.

James Okello

Grand Old Lady (Poignant Memories)

Thousands lined the quayside
As she glided into view
They disembarked her passengers
And stood off most her crew
They stripped her of her valuables
Her art and chandeliers
And as they gutted all her cabins
Her captain stood in tears

For forty years she'd plied the seas
And the oceans of this world
She'd ferried soldiers into battle
And she'd heard the guns of war
She'd carried kings and princes
To places quite unknown
Now with her pay-off pennant flying high
She leaves the place she's known as home

Her crew on board just twenty
Had rallied to the call
They'd sailed with her so many times
Now one final port of call
She's heading for the breakers yard
In a country far away
Never more to see the hills of home
Or hear the laughter every day

It was a voyage long and arduous
Just two engines not her four
She didn't have to keep to time
It didn't matter anymore
But eventually she would arrive
Off a coast she barely knew
Where the captain handed his command
To the hangman and his crew

The captain stood back on his bridge
The sun shone red and gold
She was three miles out deep in a bay
And he dreamed she'd not been sold
They coaxed her engines back to life
Bubbles formed her wake

And as her bow rose in the oily sea
Full speed she did make

Those three miles passed quite rapidly
And her bow met with the land
She rose still more to meet the shore
Then settled in the sand
And as her engines shut down one by one
Silence reigned supreme
Her plates were buckled, bent and strained
Long gone now the dream

She had sailed the oceans of the world
Was obedient to command
Once cherished much by thousands
She lies broken on the sand
Now displaced she'd be replaced
By a brand new ship and crew
And as her captain left her rusted hull
His heart was torn in two

Her time was gone but he'd move on
To command another day
Never again would he volunteer
To bring a ship into this bay
Poignant memories etched in time
His best years of command
One lasting look along the beach
To the grand old lady on the sand.

Keith Nuhrenberg-Wilson

Happiness

We sat and we talked
The old man and me,
Of life and love,
And people who see.

He talked of the woman
He'd loved through the years.
'She's gone before me,'
He said through his tears.

'But she'll be waiting
For me never fear.
We made a promise
To always stay near.

Children can hurt you
Expecting too much
When all you want
Is a smile and a touch.'

Then he looked at his dog
As it sat at his feet
'They're faithful you know,
Real hard to beat.

And the spirit you have
Will always survive
But then I've had love,'
He said with great pride.

I asked about happiness
And he looked in my eyes.
'That's something you don't
Know you have till it's gone.'

I thought on his words
As I went on my way
And decided I will be happy today.

Joan May Wills

50

Red The Rooster

He's a rakish, rowdy rooster,
A Rhode Island red.
He's so proud, his voice so loud,
It's enough to wake the dead.
So boastful, vain, has claim to fame,
He starred on the silver screen.
As herald to the Pathe News.
He took two hours to preen.
Being cock of the roost,
Needs no ego boost,
He's the stuff that men admire.
Creating for him an effigy,
On top of a cathedral spire.
Being a coxcomb with a cockscomb,
All that he can really do,
Is open this throat, strut and gloat,
Saying cock-a-doodle-do.

June Worsell

Voices Of The Rain

I've listened to the voices of the rain
And realised that heaven is not in pain

The joy I get from the rain on my face
Is just another tear put in its place

The voices are calling to one and all
We're here to help, we heard your call

Try not to be so sad we'll be gone soon
It's the time of year for the roses to bloom

We can carry your messages to those you love
We are always watching you from above

Now I stand to hear the voices of the rain
I fear them not and feel no pain.

Sharon Atkinson

Writer's Block

Writer's block is the safety of my thoughts
Where the words form before they can be caught
Where the sweetest poetry is merely a reflection
Of my inner turmoil and finest introspection

Is this for love?
Truly, I want what beats in your chest
For my own sweet music has found cardiac arrest
So we'll pump our lifeblood through the holes in our resolve
Can tragedy strike before it unfolds?

I'm scared to the core of mediocrity
But my dreams are blueprints for actuality
So fearing a fear that doesn't fear me
Seems stiflingly mediocre, albeit tinged in irony

You carry the world beneath your eyes
The oceans your tears, the land your disguise
You lack sleep, it's evident in the peaks
Of the mountains of sadness over which your tears leak

When it boils down to a chilling
Lies are for lesser poets and better villains
So I pledge the truth to you
I swear to give you your due
But the due I pledge to you may be sad as the truest truth

I'll cease to love when never becomes a memory
Such is the depth of this stimulation most sensory
When distance is a hair's breadth I'll cease to forgive
So long, goodnight, love and let live.

Justin Prinsloo

New English Verse

To make a wedding gift for you, I bring an old gift down,
a book from 1976, two years before you were born.
'The New Oxford Book of English Verse', priced – amusingly – 6 pence;
printed circa when I took my first of many unsteady steps.

Its blue case of polished Morocco is now moon pitted, scarred;
the gilt page edges thumbed to dullness in uneven marks.
Its spine is a cardboard crocodile's mouth, yawning wide,
with a sheaf of chewed up leaves torn and mangled inside.

But this is England's treasure trove – and it is treasure true –
this word hoard, inestimably precious, but not because of who
Larkin deemed were poets good enough to grace the book,
but because – back then – my dad's own unpoetic hand took

a fountain pen and wrote to my mum on the first blank page –
now surrounded by a yellow sea – tide mark of age –
'all my love' – and he signed it in the centre. Writing spare
as it is clear and sincere. Underlined, unvarnished care.

As blue and brilliant as promise and as bright as life,
his absolute affection: a heartfelt gift from man to wife.
All his love, duly rendered, daily, yearly, without fanfare.
Always current as the day he wrote it, whenever I read it there.

So these are my words too, not new, but only now to you confessed.
Here is all my love in writing, and this ink is always fresh.

Laurence Cooper

My Beard

Loyalty is
Crawling back,
Knowing full well
That I'll hurt you again.
And you do it
Every time.
Why?
I want you in my life,
Until I get bored
And mutilate you.
I, a selfish,
Ungrateful man,
Deserve far worse
Than you.

You're all that I am not,
Rough to the eye,
Soft to the touch,
Full of wisdom,
Void of harm.
You're the mask
I hide behind,
Deluding,
Deceiving,
Convincing
All who look that I
Am all that you are.

I'm a charlatan,
You're a guide.
You're a sage,
I'm a child.
I spit venom,
You give praise.
You lead,
And I manipulate.

I drag you down,
You raise me up.
I taint your grace,
You lend me some.

I wound you,
You heal us both
And forgive me
Every time.

I'm a lost cause,
Holding you back,
So why stay by
My side?

Kieran Kejiou

From The Heart

(For My Best Friend Marina, Always)

I want your arms around me,
With your lips locked on mine.
You inspire me to want to be better,
And that everything will be fine.

You can get my heart racing,
With your captivating charm.
Whenever I think about you,
I get an electrifying feeling, all up my arm.

You make everything look easy,
In each and every way.
I could easily fall in love with you,
Deeper with each day.

You are as talented as Shakespeare,
As enchanting as the sea.
Wherever you are in the world,
Is where I want to be.

I've had these feelings for years,
You didn't even know.
That all I've ever wanted to do,
Is never let you go.

Chloe Catlin

Jazz In The Evening

Do you remember when the saxophone played,
and your feet dipped and swayed
with the same rhythm as mine?
Remember how my hand traipsed your waist
and you leaned into it, wasting no time
as the drums licked the skins,
our skins licking the sweat off of each other
as we held close while the beat slowed down to a tick-tock tempo.
The piano guided our steps underneath the blue lighted setting,
and when we closed our eyes our other senses were heightened -
touch speaking more than our tongues ever could,
sound allowing us to see more than we ever would
without the blessing of jazz in its purest form.
As we waded through life's storm
made peaceful by the gift of Quiet Storm.
The Blues were our muse, our feet were our brushes
and we painted all night long.
Hiking up your dress to perform long strokes on the dance floor,
we dabbed our heels and the balls of our feet in the ink and on to the canvas,
leaving behind the moment in time where our souls were joyous.
The Blues were our muse and we would dance
long after the music had stopped,
creating our art to the sound of the morning thrushes.
We stepped non-stop to the beat of our hearts,
our movements in our space a contemporary art,
they were hard to comprehend, but easier to appreciate.
Never did the music attempt to negate
the heat within our stare,
always laissez-faire.
Even when I'm alone,
memories of you in jazz
always finds a way
to keep you near.
Remember how my hand traipsed your waist
and you leaned into it, showing no hesitation
as the drums licked the skins.
Remember how your palms were sweating
with anticipation,
and how you wasted no time in making a correlation

between the twang of the guitar
and the movement of your feet and arms.
That night the spirits of B.B. King, Ray Charles and Miles Davis
evoked the musical passions within us that were innate for eons
so that we could save this
moment and all others like it,
tattooed on the history of we black people.
The moon danced in the light of the sun,
I danced in the light of your countenance
and you danced in the light of the Blues.
While you were caught up in the many hues,
which were construed oftentimes as rage and pain
for the years lain as slaves,
I watched on as you illustrated that through dance,
we pave our way to inner peace -
tapping, stepping, spinning and dipping
to an evening time jazz piece.

Aiden Harmitt-Williams

Sink Or Swim

My eyes swim until I can't see,
and my head drowns with thoughts
that long to anchor me.
Like fish hooks caught tenderly beneath my skin,
with every second passing I'm reeled closer in.
The future becomes darker with every held breath,
as I sink further below to be lost within its depths.

Wynona Lodge

Dedicated To The One I Love

I have always struggled with those three little words,
But with you it feels so natural,
Like it is meant to be,
Nothing forced but something so actual.

Those words I even find hard to say to my family,
It's like I have the words ready to say . . .
But then there seems to be an internal barrier,
Just something in the way.

To have the sentiment not returned,
Really did hurt.
My heart had been ripped out and smeared through the metaphorical dirt . . .

Now I can share this sentiment once again,
And it feels so right to say it to you.
I now feel able to say it to friends and family,
Sharing this emotion is no longer an issue.

I thank you for this and so much more . . .
You were the missing piece,
The piece which my heart will always beat for . . .

I love you.

Lauren Saunby

Friend Or Foe?

Standing face to face
Alone, the two of us
You stand proud and tall
I feel tiny and small

I'm dressed in dirt and cloths
You're in khaki, wielding your sword
Your eyes are burning
Is it pity?
Is it hate?

As the world around us stops
And everything crumbles
You stand proud and tall
I feel tiny and small

I look into your eyes
Pleading, I drop to my knees
No monsoon compares
To the volume of my tears
Is it working?

Your eyes are burning
Are you a friend
Or are you a foe?

Your sword sparkles in the sunlight
Ready to attack

As you stand tall
I pray you'll spare my soul.

Dess Ander

Once A Place In The Country

There had been little movement for some time,
We were truly stuck, a summer traffic jam
Stretching into the distance almost as far
As the eye could see, a meandering line
Of vehicles, wedged like sardines in a can,
Immobilised, miles of combusting motor cars.

Half a century ago, this arterial road feeding
A sprawling network of tree-lane motorways
Was then a path, a capillary decked in green,
Winding and hedge-lined, a track leading
Into a world without noise, a special place
Where air tasted fresh, and smelled so clean.

It was possible, then, to wander and wallow
Amid wafting scents and sounds, to relax completely
And to feel a part of Mother Nature's grand plan,
To discreetly approach, undetected, some sleepy hollow,
Whose inhabitants, undisturbed, continued to sing sweetly,
Or nibble neatly, unaffected by the presence of mere Man.

But it was the butterflies, always fluttering free,
Colourful wraithes floating in flight between patches
Of rambling purple vetch that caught the eye,
Darting will-o'-the-wisps, so lovely to see,
Blues, Brimstone Yellows with shimmering splashes
Of iridescence, and wings almost too fragile to fly.

Occasionally, some artist would grace the scene,
Capturing on canvas, these butterflies that danced
Lightly, upon a summer breeze, unafraid and so carefree,
Preserving the flavour of what once had been,
Of beauty on the wing and nature in balance,
A permanence in oils, reserved for posterity.

And now, that living landscape has gone,
Swallowed up by passing time and regurgitated
Later, as a bleak and grey industrial sprawl,
Hedgerows, trees or fields, there are none,
Only factories, and concrete chimneys, erect, naked,
Emitting death as a choking sulphurous pall.

Suddenly there was a movement in the line at last,
And the urgent noise of engines revving hard
Contrasts starkly with the unhurried flight
Of a solitary butterfly, lazily zig-zagging past,
Symbolising the legacy that progressive Man has ignored,
Transcending time, a beautiful staccato-dancing Cabbage White.

Andrew Farmer

The Blackthorn, The Briar And The Rose

At the headland of a meadow long since passed o'er by time,
There once held court, three Musketeers of sort, their roots and arms entwined.
They discuss the passing seasons poetry and prose,
Neither lords of withy nor coppice, the Blackthorn, the Briar and the Rose.
They grew about, a royal though youthful oak with strength and beauty spare,
His mantle bore them shelter, all who dwelt around him there.
Beneath his boughs upon the green, a ploughman held a village wench,
Drinking with lust her ruby lips, with thirst he n'er would quench.
But the hands of time will wait for none, and change a long march made,
For the ploughman was taken a soldier, fodder for cannon and blade.
The maid died young for her awful loss still pure as a morning dove,
And the rose became a token of her truest dearest love.
The briar became a fine gentleman's cane, the blackthorn a calabash stem,
With only a thought for their beauty by those who slaughtered them.
The youthful oak they grew about, the keel of a galleon cast.
Lay seven leagues beneath the waves these four hundred years now passed.
Gone are the ruby red lips, the hand that would guide the plough,
The blackthorn, the briar, the oak and the rose, for all are sleeping now.
So grasp each day and use it well, consider thyself most blessed,
For though the morrow surely comes t'well maybe one ye'll not possess.

Kevin F Dunn

Homelessness

Am I invisible to you all?
Why am I an object of ridicule and hate?
I sit here on the streets day after day,
I occupy various spots from dawn, till dusk and until very late.
'Get a job you lazy b*****d,' someone screams at me,
I did have one though a long time ago,
But the recession destroyed my life,
I was crushed with an almighty financial blow.
I've ended up on the streets now for a couple of years,
Winter months are the worst as I battle against the frost and snow,
The homeless shelters are kind to me with their warm meals and Xmas gifts,
How many more years will I be homeless – I don't know?
My homeless friends are from every race and nation on Earth,
London is a city divided by class and wealth,
Life on the streets is not for the faint-hearted,
As homeless folk struggle at times with their health.
My life is slowly improving now,
I work for the Big Issue part-time,
With their help I now have a roof over my head,
A life off the streets is now mine.

Fine Buliciri

Elegy In A Scrap Yard 2

(Apologies To Thomas Grey)

A klaxon sounds the knell of the parting day.
The billowing winds blow the remnants of sodden news away
Which lodge amongst the rusted axles and cylinder heads
And twisted frames and iron bedsteads,
Where once naked forms writhed with passion.
Coiled rusty hawsers, shackles, hooks and stanchions
Entangled in a crazy metal labyrinth of hissing pipes
And tarred snaking hoses that wrap around and strangle
Cans and drums with barbed wire entangles.
Black volcanic eruptions of smouldering lava
Obsidian monument to Man's ingenuity and obsolescence.
Recycle the cycle, reincarnate the Aga.
Despite the wrecking ball and snarling grab
The phoenix of peace will rise in our prayers
And fill the yard with oaken ploughshares.
The mangy shepherd dogs prowl like drones
The weary labourer trudges his funereal way home
Will tomorrow be a lighter load
Or will his burden be forever on the Sisyphus Road?

David Birtwistle

The Visit

The door locked behind me as I entered the psychiatric ward,
  Immediately I was thrown into a world of human tragedy,
Elderly patients confronted me,
  Their bodies distorted with mental and physical disabilities,
Unable even to attend their normal bodily functions,
  Hopefully for most, unaware of the indignities life had
Bestowed upon them.

Devoted staff running around, reassuring the visitors,
  Making life as comfortable as possible in this sad situation,
Relatives trying to coax some form of recognition
  From these once brilliant people.
Reluctant to come to terms with the inevitable,
  Knowing that the spark that once lit the face
Of a loved one had gone forever.

On walking out into the sunshine,
  A voice said, and how do you feel?
With tears streaming down my face. I likened
It to a battlefield, with no winners,
For the enemy was a cruel disease that had
Afflicted them.
I walked on feeling full, so full,
  Full of emptiness, home, to the
Comfort of my living.

Gladys C'Ailceta

To Tom (Laura's Reply)

My heart is really aching
Each and every day
As I write this letter
As I find the words to say

You fought your battle well my dear
Your death is a black cloud
I find it hard without you
But I'm so immensely proud

Your son is growing up now
He asks me where you are
I don't know what to tell him
Are you near or far?

As I sit by your coffin
How I miss your face
Now there's a big void in my heart
That no one will ever replace

We were getting married
My heart was going to sing
But now that's all gone
I'll never wear your ring

So goodbye my one true hero
You served your country well
All your family miss you
We ring the final bell.

Lee Rowley

Flying With The Music

Shattered into pieces, falling down the abyss, no bottom, no end,
Broken in many ways, will I ever mend?
Music, lovingly held my hand, and said, 'I will always be your friend . . .
I know the language that holds people together
So get up, stay with me, and you will smile forever . . .'

But,
I am not just the sounds that bring you lots of pleasure,
So you can play your records, whatever the weather,
Dancing chords of delight, minds reaching an octave higher
Our voice soaring with the notes, happiness we remember,

So
You think you've been broken, you think you've been hurt
You think you are stamped right down in the dirt
Well, each little piece of you, that you thought was going to rust,
Was actually a little note at rest, gathering a little bit of dust

A broken heart that is in little pieces
Are words of a new song for new concerts and releases
Music came and told me this first thing in the morning
As when I woke, I had a brand new feeling, dawning
My pieces had been rearranged
Like a new symphony, had been explained,
An orchestra of angels, lifted me high, with sonorous wings
As a great powerful firebird, but who gently sings

We flew over the rooftops and colourful valleys all night,
Music travels, passes through walls, when there is no sight
Some people shouted, 'Will you turn that down, I can't get to sleep.'
But I carried on flying over cities, and graveyards, without getting the creeps

Hoards of people were lying in their beds
Torn from many countries, their hearts having bled
But they still sing, they still dance
They are safe with me the music, they have a chance

I am not just the sounds that sing out from the telly
I get boxed, packaged and sold into something smelly
But actually

I am freedom
I can't be tamed
I am everywhere

I am not ashamed
I move around in the air
I can touch you, when you're not there
I make you feel alive, yes you do still care
I am music
I am free
Welcome back to humanity.

Rachel Arnold

Home Alone

I sit at home
All alone
No one there
The house is dark
I'm frightened
There's no electricity
Mum's not paid the bill again
But, still I wish she was here
All I can see are the empty bottles
On the table, standing like statues
Then the clock strikes twelve
Mum is still not back
Once again
Mum's drinking again
it's not fair this life
It cannot be safe for me
For I am only nine
I find it hard
Because my father left
Some time ago
He tried but couldn't stop
Mum from drinking
So once again I'm home alone
Living the pain and loneliness
With the bottles on the table
Just staring back at me
The lamp post outside is
My guiding star.

Thomas Sims

For Mum

No more you sit beside my bed to pray,
To talk with you would take all pain away,
You left me, not a single word you said,
To soften all the anguish in my head.
I often think about you for a while,
I think of all your ways and softly smile,
You still bring all the joy you did before,
And all the warmth inside, and maybe more.
To see your face beside me at your best,
When I am weary and in need of rest,
Makes all the world seem right and surely true;
For I am standing proud, right next to you.

I see you frown, I see it in your face;
That down-turned mouth just cannot be displaced.
I come to you and place my hand in yours,
The tears you cry dry up and cease to pour.
You thank me, unsure whether I am there,
You smile and stretch your legs out on the chair,
Enjoy the hairs now raised upon your back,
Your eyes now closed to hear the voice life lacks.
I cannot speak, I only come to pray;
To comfort, as in life, but not to stay,
But all the world is right and surely true,
While I am standing proud, right next to you.

Ruth Cooke

Lonesome Statue

I stand alone so still and silent
Please notice me I'm here defiant
You look and gaze but see through me
I look back to you and wish I was free
I quiver silently as I feel the trickle of rain
Please come and stand by me again
Many pass and look away
I'm here, don't ignore, please come and stay
My molten body burns in the midday sun
Please give me shelter this isn't much fun
Click, click, the deafening sound I hear
I wish my face could change just to make you fear
You swing on me and laugh aloud
Hey! Get off me, get back in the crowd
The night draws in and the darkness comes down
A torch shines bright to light up my frown
All alone again with my thoughts I think
What must it be like to even take a drink
The moment of stillness, the sound of the night
The feeling of loneliness comes to give me a fright
I freely stand so tall for all to see
I am a lonesome statue so please don't pity me.

Donna-Marie Whatmore

Listen . . .

Listen!
Can you hear the roar?
Of ten thousand shells,
A battle cry,
As they fight,
Hold their corner,
Exhausted,
But carried on the moment,
Trained to do their bit,
Born to die young,
Smeared in dirt,
Each other's blood,
Last breath taken in a distant land,
The dream of adventure,
A sour note.

I hear the roar of ten thousand shells,
Standing among a sea of white memorials,
Heart pounding,
I feel the earth shake beneath my feet,
Smell the gas,
Listen to the screams,
My vision overcast, blood-red.

Vivid as if it was yesterday,
Jostling for position in the trenches,
I slide in the mud,
I have brushed a face,
Realise with a shock it matches,
The sepia photograph, but blood-red.

Reaching through the generations,
A cool hand takes mine,
I am aghast with grief,
For a man I know only by name,
Long-chiselled on a village cenotaph,
My tears fall like the rain, but blood-red.

I am back in that quiet place,
The only sound is my own voice,
But it is a voice that must be heard,
I cry out for peace,
Standing among a sea of white memorials,
Arms aloft in my dress, blood-red.

Joy Edwards

Forbidden Love

Hidden secrets
Secret smiles
Smiles hidden
Truth forbidden
Forbidden love
Love secrets
Secret smiles
Smiles hidden
Hidden secrets
Locked tight
Strongest tension
Strangling tight
Tight emotion
Emotion hidden
Secret smiles
Smiles forbidden
No compromise
Given.

Gillian Sims

The Gallery

Eyesight failing he peers at the black box in the corner of his room
Its flickering and fast moving pictures blurred and brash
The dialogue confusing and incomprehensible
Isn't there a war on? He muses
Irritated, he flicks a switch and makes it disappear

His rheumy eyes steady on his deckle edge photographs
Though faded and sepia, these are motionless, comforting
A tiny spark ignites, a lost memory moves to the fore
A woman's hand, a smile – was there a kiss?
He gazes down, twists a gold band on his wizened finger

But where is she now . . . the one whose name eludes him?
She keeps watch over him with such familiarity; a lost relative perhaps?
The next image, a young man's eyes shine sharp and bright
Intuitively he knows the uniform is green, wearily he stands to form a salute
And with unfamiliar clarity, recites an army name and rank

He strains to focus while his brain snags on faded thoughts
From another picture, the girl smiles and holds a tiny form
Cosseted, the infant sleeps contentedly in her arms
He can't quite be certain . . . that she once held him?
Yes he recollects, she embraced him too, loved him with all her heart!

Her hair was auburn and shone like burnished copper
And her nose was dappled with the lightest of freckles
His fingers once brushed her hair off her pink blushed cheeks
He makes a mental note to enquire; but who would he ask?
Nobody calls by these days

Shuffling, and with arthritic hands he turns to the radio for comfort
An old familiar tune begins to resonate in his head
Triggers another acquainted pathway long since burnt out
Her name percolates and forms in his cracked, dry mouth
Eyes closed, he smiles and whispers it aloud

Once more he hears her sweet voice clear inside his aged mind
Haunting, it appeals, beautiful like a tender lullaby
For certain it fine tunes his senses now
Tears brim, like salty jewels washing his tide of grief
My beloved, the Blitz took you both, keep waiting, I'm nearly home.

Julie Alexandra Povall

A Million Thoughts To Last A Lifetime

Sometimes I sit, wonder and think,
How the time literally flies by within a blink.
Why the clock ticks and makes the sound it does,
Who inspired the creator, was that a must?
Sometimes I wonder, sit and think,
How the world travels, but stays in sync.
With the emotions and daily feelings of those who walk this earth,
How it influences the change of environment, and it touches people's nerves.
Momentarily I sit, think and wonder,
How it appears to be humankind putting people under.
Why there is war, and youngsters fighting against each other,
But when will there be a day, that they fight for one another.
Society today is filled with neglect, division and fear,
When will it be replaced with unity, peace and care.
The consistent downpour of negativity, exploding through the news,
But this, if we could, is not something we would want to choose.
The daily movements, the consistent battle to live each day, comes with rules
and regulations we must obey.
But why should we confine our lives to a box, and lead by someone else's
mind.
Instead of travelling the path set out for every individual to find?
We live to boundaries, instead of limits.
But there are no limits, so why don't we live by the power of the never-ending
visions and dreams?

Vanessa Henderson

Bluebell

A lonely bluebell beneath the canopy; growing silent, shaded, alone.
Nettles surround her from each direction, trying to stop her, shadow her, break
  her.
Desperate to grow strong and tall, bloom in the sun, see the light.
You won't keep this bluebell down. She will live. She will grow. She will shine.

An enduring bluebell, sat indomitably in the sunbeams; growing strong,
beautiful, free.

Christina Marshall

Fantasia

The day was bright and crisp with chilly ice blue skies. Perfect. Only last week the forecast had been for warm sunny conditions with a Met Office amber melt warning. The inhabitants of Cacao were in a frenzy of excitement. Today was the wedding of Prince Toblerone from Switzerland and their own Princess Praline. The M&M family and their cousins, the Smarties, who had travelled up on the tube were already in position along Quality Street, awaiting the procession which would pass by them on its way down the mall to Westminstrel Abbey. The security police, the Mall Teasers, lined the highway to control the crowd of Assortments that packed the pavements layer upon layer. The city clock chimed eleven o'clock and the mall was alive with music as the massed bands led by the Mars Brigade resplendent in their orange and brown coats, followed by the Yorkies in their rich blue livery, marched majestically onto the Abbey, passing by the Chocolate Fountain, the scene of so many historical Celebrations and Revels. The royal coach, carrying Princess Praline and her father, set off from Magnum Palace to join the procession at Rollo Park, adorned in gold leaf and pulled by six now white horses, beautifully groomed and braided with dazzling multicoloured ribbons. The following coach carried other members of the royal family, notably the Truffles, including the Princesses Vienna, Cappuccino, Champagne and Marzipan. The Assortments gasped in admiration at their elegant cream and beige flowing gowns topped with crystallised tiaras. The outriders, The Crunchies, however drew the biggest cheer with their gold and crimson swirling capes and glittering sabres. They were at their crispiest and snappy best.

At the Abbey, Prince Toblerone had already arrived with his family and entourage. He proceeded through the packed congregation with his best man, Kit, the eldest of the Kit-Kat dynasty, majestic in his red and silver tunic. They acknowledged the rows of supporters from abroad; the Lindts, the Ferrero Rochers and the towering Profiteroles from Switzerland; the Guylians and Bourbon Liquers from France; and the Delightful Turkish contingent. Finally from South America, the Brazils, who were there amongst some controversy. There had been some unsavoury gossip surrounding the family, some talk of human rights abuses, rumours of shelling and bean torture, in fact they were regarded as a little insane, nutty in fact. They had left a bitter taste.

Princess Praline arrived with her father and they joined Toblerone at the altar where they were greeted by Archbishop Cadbury who took the wedding vows. The hymns and anthems were carried by the acoustics to every vault and niche of that great auditorium. The lesson was read by Bishop Fry, who took his passage from The Fair Trade Bible, the text being from Galaxions and

its message of sharing and sacrifice. The sermon was delivered by Bishop Rowntree on the theme of sweetness, fusion and harmony. The couple finally embraced and emerged from the Abbey to roars of approbation from the congregation.

The Cheerios followed them onto the Abbey steps where the vast Assortments were waiting to welcome them. A huge wall of sound from the bell tower arose with a tumultuous peal of joy and celebration. The M&Ms cheered as they never had before. The television company TW9 (commonly known as Twix) were there in force of course to record the occasion for posterity. As they were about to leave an ugly group of protesters had gathered by the corner. They were the Boiled Sweet Gang from the Black Magic suburb of East Cacao. The militant arm were represented by the hooded Bulls' Eyes backed up by the Acid Drops and Humbugs. They waved anti-monarch banners and things looked to turn nasty until a platoon of Crunchie boys intervened and moved them on to be thrown into the litter bins and to the mercy of the Walnut Whips. 'Fancy having a Boiled Sweet as president,' said Mrs M&M. Mr M&M gave out a huge guffaw and the rest of the Assortments laughed and Snickered.

At last the party were ready to travel onto Magnum Palace for the reception and presentation on the balcony. The Mars Band and Yorkies headed the parade once again and everyone followed behind to mass outside the Palace. Meanwhile inside the great hall a royal banquet had been prepared. Caramel soup for starters followed by tasty pies and honey dips, fruits from around the world and delicacies too numerous to mention, all efficiently served by the royal catering company, Fingers and Teacakes. The master of ceremonies Mr Orange guided the proceedings seamlessly, segment by segment, through the speeches and presentations. Finally it was time to greet the Assortments on the balcony.

The doors swung open and the royal party assembled together and as the bride and groom shared a loving embrace to the roar of the assembled Assortment, a spectacular fly past swooped over the whole gathering led by the brilliant Aeros in their striking formation and acrobatics. Their vapour trails had hardly evaporated when the sky was suddenly illuminated by a lightning flash of neon light as rockets pierced the gathering dusk, followed by a shower of gold and silver stars. A cascade of fireworks exploded in a maelstrom of pyrotechnics. All around was a crescendo of noise, hisses and cracks like thunder in a complete Fantasia. At every Starburst, the Assortments cheered until eventually all that remained was a billowy pall of smoke as the royal party left the balcony with a wave and a flourish.

The M&M family and the Smarties wended their way home, each lost in a world of their own, shuffling through the rainbow-coloured Assortment wrappers that swirled around their feet. 'Well what did you make of that for a

day out young Purple?' said Mr M&M.
Purple M&M gazed up wistfully into the night sky at the Milky Way. 'It was... It
was simply Flaketastic!' she said in a Wispa.

Hayes Turner

Tell It

I alter the story
Every time
The tale of how you
Were and were not mine.
You were and were not mine.

Amicable parting
Or abandonment
Miles or inches between
What was heard and what was meant.

We are martyrs, heroes, lovers, losers,
Villains, victims, beggars, choosers.
It is all true
And it is all a lie
Take the what and who
Fill in the how and why.

Whichever way I say it
Whichever way I sell it
I never get our story right.

I think that's why I tell it.

Billie Erin Morley Heath

At The Street Fair

We're selling my old toys today.

Mum made a sign last night. 'Fill a bag for £2'.

'You don't need those old things anymore,' she told me, 'and we need the money.'

We always seem to need money these days.

She's talking to an old lady with a stick.

I watch her pass my pink elephant over the stall. I tug at her arm.

'Don't sell Nelly,' I whisper.

'Not now Maisey,' she says.

I sit back on the grass, annoyed, and open my lunch box – juice, brown bread sandwiches and a wrinkly old apple. Boring! But then I spot my dad, near the hot dog van. He's sitting on the wall with his 'new family', eating ice cream. I wish I could live with my dad too.

Mum hasn't seen him yet, but he's seen me. He says something to his girlfriend and stands up. He's coming over.

He does a funny dance for me as he passes the men in straw hats, playing music. Dad always makes me laugh. But it's Mum that sits on my bed after he's gone and cuddles me if I cry. Why can't we all live together, like we used to?

I jump up to meet him. He tries to ruffle my hair but I grab his hand and lead him to our stall. Mum is still talking. She doesn't notice me reaching out.

I squeeze both their hands tight.

Now I remember how it feels.

I hold my breath and wish.

Maia Cornish

All Kinds Of Love

True love – spirit of the heart.
Magical emotion which can tear one's world apart.
Eternal devotion – tender and true
Caring, unbelievable, treasuring you!
Love for a woman or maybe a man.
Love for a child – since the world first began.
Love for God's creatures, furry and small,
The sea and the mountains and wild birds' call.
Love of the flowers, the trees and the sky.
Love just of living as time passes by.
The stars in the heavens sparkling and bright
Reflect in the eyes which shine with love's light.
The love and the passions of youthful dreams
Turn to gold embers where aged ones lean.
But forget not our Maker and answer His call
For He gave unto us the greatest love of them all.

Enid Hewitt

Moon Glow

Honey blossom smile from youth's sweet chamber of dreams,
Casts out all fears and doubts,
In cornflower blue eyes,
Through slumber and in peace,
Not worldly wise,
But innocent as a dove
Up high in the blossom tree,
She flies so true like a zephyr in the sky so free.
Brave moon in your silent space,
You wear no satin or expensive lace,
Though your light is as pure as gold.
Once a young gem, melting in the heat of the sun,
Now showing your age,
You're getting old, dry dust upon your brow,
And silver in your face.

T.J. Bailey

Photo ID

Excuse me – I'm sorry to bother you.
Have you seen this girl?
She'll be twenty now.
She was twelve when this was taken.
That's the last time I saw her smile.
That's the last time I saw her.
I don't think that she's dead,
because I can still feel her flickering,
sometimes, inside me
– a candle flame not quite snuffed out.

The irony is that she was fleeing abuse
when she was abducted,
shoplifted from life and then milked
for money through sex-work.
There's not much of her left
– the girl in the photo – me.
I wish I knew a safe place
or a safe face to show her to. Please –
can you still see her, a little?
Would you help me to find her?
Will you help me?
Will you?

Cathy Bryant

The Miracle

Tea was ready, Sarah looked to the headland where two figures were silhouetted against the setting sun. They had been standing vigil every waking moment since the crabbers had reported their father's boat had last been seen drifting into St Catherine's Sound. The adults knew there was not much hope but the two boys would not have it and kept watching for him.
As Sarah watched, the two figures took off, running excitedly downhill towards the harbour. Miracles do happen, badly damaged their father had limped home.

Jaz (Janet Collins)

If

Sit and stare,
Looking, but not seeing,
Thinking of nothing,
Wondering, not doing,
Twiddling thumbs, wasting time,
Sitting the day away.

Cleaning the floor,
Walking to school,
Avoiding hazards along the way,
Collecting rubbish, to earn a crust,
Cutting hands,
Finding dirty water to drink.

Walking, doing nothing,
Sitting drinking coffee,
Playing on the phone,
Chatting to friends,
Shopping for clothes,
Having lunch, relaxing.

Searching for food,
No clothes to wear,
Working the land,
From dawn to dusk,
Mud huts crowded,
No parents to help.

Going to work,
Planning a holiday,
Earning a wage,
For plenty to share,
Moaning about the weather,
And paying a bill.

No shoes, no home,
Slumped in a factory,
Sewing a dress,
For you to wear,
Little hands sore,
Working for our pleasure.

If the world was different,
Would we care?
If no food, no water, no toilet,
Would we care?
If no wage, no home,
Would we care?
If no more of anything,
Would we care?

Gail Underwood

Extract From (As Yet) Untitled Novel

Tierney faltered. There was no going back from what she was about to do. Once she entered the unassuming little café, her life was going to change immeasurably forever. That in itself wasn't what she found so daunting, after all, her life had taken a great many turns far more remarkable than this. But after today everyone would know about them. All the elements of her extraordinary life up to this point had been known to only a select few. From this moment on her secrets would no longer be her own. She rolled her shoulders slowly, feeling all her worries slide off them and into the road behind her. And with a surprising sense of purpose she gave the door a firm nudge and stepped inside.

As her eyes adjusted to the dim light tarnished with steam from the coffee machine and smoke from the poky little open kitchen, she glanced around the room, knowing exactly what she was looking for. Another enthusiastic and nervous young woman, much as she had once been herself, probably far too over dressed for the venue with over-straightened hair, some hideous fat-free-super-skinny-no-cream-no-sugar-no-fun black coffee clutched in one hand, unorganised notes and a pen in the other, with an untouched plate of biscuits at her side. Her eyes came to rest on a twenty-something woman hunched over a small table in the window. The young woman looked up and their eyes met. Tierney smiled to herself. She could not have been more right.

Serenity Rose

Love

All's fair in love and war,
Really!
You miss the point.
War is love
Mated with spite.
And love,
True love,
Is all about sacrifice.
Know the ecstasy
Of that moment
In birth
When you fall in love with your child.
When giving your life is a given,
It's all about the sacrifice.
When you meet
Your mate
And in that moment
Your soul cries out,
'I want to make you happy.'
That's what it's all about.
In a world where shallow
Self-obsess
Has gained a mastery,
How can such
Know of love
When their greed is all for *ME*.
Love is living,
Breathing,
Vibrant,
Like energy, best shared.
When love becomes a cul-de-sac
It festers there.
Maslow's twisted mind
Made selfishness our share.
Now that selfishness
Has stopped the flow,
We lack the power of love.
Whoever made sex
The apse of love,

Has never known love's touch.
Asexual is not loveless
In them pure love abides.
The love of a child for a parent,
The love of a caring friend.
Love for God in a sunset
Or a gentle saving hand.
Mother's love lasts longest,
Transcends the bonds of time,
But even now endangered
By Maslow's selfish climb.
This dark matter of self love
Creeps in a rising tide,
It bubbles up from cul-de-sacs,
Those death-like no through roads.
We need to staunch this flow.
And in committed attitude
Give faithful rise to love,
True love,
Pure love,
Devoted, vigorous, vital,
Unswerving power of love.
Love is living,
Breathing,
Vibrant,
Like energy, best shared.

Patricia-Ann Stone

A Collapse

Throwback to
the moon shining barely; a reminder of
unconnected pieces missing –

a sudden rush of adrenaline

Red wine spilled on the carpet; hatred
Arguments lost in your head; imagined
Illusion of ultimate desire; trashed
Phrases; unfinished

Being a raven; white
It is not out of norm but questions survival
leaving a nest; pushed away
a collapse,
how to hit (almost) the ground?

Drops of rain falling down on the paper,
inability to stretch wings
inability to

be

Windows falling; inside
the cage

The very same obsessions of a human
being
equivalent to an outcast

Impression of the reality
swallowed by the deep sea
a total blackout; the age of innocence
lost
found
los-
t

And when I paid you back that time, I paid you double.

I didn't choose this, Dad, it chose me,
I don't want to be trapped, I want to be free,
I didn't expect you to be happy or glad,
But it's the way it is, I'm sorry, Dad.

I hope, one day, you'll understand,
And you'll look me in the eye and shake my hand,
cos I only ever wanted you to be proud of me, Dad,
Proud that I'm your son,
Your special lad.

Jackie Knowles

The Demon Inside

As I opened my eyes, dark black pupils stared back at me. I was sweating and shaking, this thing was laughing, grinning at me with the smile of a Joker. Teeth bared like a dog, their tongue tipped at the edges, flicking it around fangs that were protruding from the tops of its gums. I screamed and this thing quickly cupped my mouth with its hands, pushing me harder into my bed.

'Hush, girl. I wouldn't do that.' It hissed those words more so than spoke them. My mind raced with the endless thoughts of what was going to happen to me. Was I going to die like this? Alone, helpless and at the hands of a demon? Tears streamed my face, I was so scared. I closed my eyes, shoulders shaking with my silent, flowing tears and incomprehensible fear that was coursing through my body.

Just then I felt the ground beneath me shaking, convulsing like the body of the dead when being re-animated. I dared open my eyes, I saw its eyes glaring back at me and wished I hadn't opened them. The demon was shaking, its shoulders lurching back and forward, its face scrunched up in pain, then there was a loud, sharp crack and a squeal and an explosion of blood. Its head fell forward and it was laughing. Behind it, appeared two wings, one black and made of scales and the other white and made of feathers.

A demon or an angel...

Kaylee Branch

Musings From A Dark Poet

You are as dark as an alter-ego.
Your eyes are windowless
Because your soul fled long ago
From all who tried to love you

Your smile is saccharine
The sweetness replaced by E numbers
Tasty for seconds but false
The aftertaste too acerbic

Your make-up masks the lines of discontent upon your brow
The bitterness mars your once plump lips
Kissable no longer
At least not by me

Instead of mellowing like a fine wine
In your impatience, you used immature berries
And your brew became toxic
Lethal to all who sip from your poison chalice

Your mansion is devoid of love
No fledglings share your nest
Teaching them to fly
Would have cost you effort

There are cracks in your foundation
The ugliness you seek to camouflage
Is seeping through
Plain for all to see now

You demanded gratitude for your attention
Whilst isolating me from all I held dear
The pedestal you created for others to worship you
Has fractured from the weight of your ego.

Leevi Armas Seppänen

Blurred Lines

To hear nothing is very extreme . . .
It means that the brain has switched to another level
Could it be the silence within a dream
Or something beyond understanding – the Devil

To hear nothing in an extreme dream,
When the brain switches to another state
Makes the body feel weightless, almost like flight
Your brain is cocooned, you must not fight.

Only a certain noise pitch in an extreme dream,
Slowly wakens the brain from its mezzanine.
Eyes open wide, slumber a distant sheen
Disorientated, confused, reality or a dream?

Caterina Servadei

What's Left

When it was sunset then summer then sunrise all in one day
And it seemed the grass grew to our throats all in that day
You brought me a goat by a rope, straight to the back door, up a set of
wooden steps.

You sang me a song about a diamond ring
I waited on the porch steps for what seemed days and hours
but was just hours.

We wore such heavy coats even in summer then
That, or nothing at all it seemed, our toes grown black by August
We were like goats.

A few trees, a house, some long grass, some old photos
Diamond rings on all our fingers.

Robin Pridy

A Terminator's Meander V2.3

I'm settling down to a cruising speed,
living in overdrive settles the need,
to dismiss the decreed,
agreed belief,
seeds planted,
guaranteed,
to be granted,
relief,
sticking to a canter.
Like a horse of course,
my own recourse;
to the unknown,
balancing force,
that since I've been in pants short,
has not yet chosen to retort.
I don't try to distort,
the thought,
and clarity of the chaos report,
that is my life in short.

I'm operating on high levels of trust and disbelieving,
concealing my ill feeling and general displeasing, demeanour is truly
revealing,
my inner workings giving debriefings,
therapists chitter-chatter.
Improve the matter between your ears,
kill fears with a good natter,
beers and choice of food platters.
It matters,
to see a positive outlook,
don't duck,
your responsibilities,
become unstuck
and run amok.
Pluck the courage to be a hero.
Zero in on the dinero
and you'll go Emperor Nero;

berseko! Reversal of fortunes,
wheels of Boethius,
ought to,
cast you back round,
mining the fierro.

Adam Pinwill

Untitled

Have you ever had the time to think clearly in your head
How about wishing you wouldn't wake up from your bed.

Have you ever felt so depressed that even with a big chocolate bar
Your endorphins will be suppressed.

Lying here now. Wishing life was new,
Where seizures didn't happen, where my voice was on cue.

But no, it takes me every day away.
Out of the room, out of my mind. Into an out of body sensation you find.

No one can say, oh I know how you feel,
It can't be nice, not even to go out for a meal.

Sitting there quietly enjoying the food, then the brain clicks into a mood.
It tells you I want to make you look like a fool. I'm going to ruin it for all.

Peek-a-boo, I'm still here, I'm never going to disappear.

So when I say to you, have you ever felt this way?
I'm not blaming you, I'm just saying that you don't know how I feel.
So all I can do is write it down to show you that what I go through is real.

So when you see someone struggling some way, having a seizure shaking away.
Please step back and silently pray, that they will come to an end someday.

Rebecca Hughes

Fugitive On The Run

I'm a fugitive on the run
Trying to dodge the missiles and gun
I'm a man without a country
No safe place, no entry
An alien in my own home

A rebel with just cause
I stand for freedom and equality
Not unfairness and brutality
I stand for those without a voice
Those denied the right to be happy and rejoice
Or the freedom to make a choice

I shudder at those who carry out executions
I quiver at those who carry out electrocutions
How can they feel it just to persecute
Those who have nothing and are destitute

I am a peaceful activist with truth in my heart
For those whose lives have been ripped apart
For those who live in fear
And wait each day for their loved ones to appear
Despite the futility of the act

I champion free speech
Abhor those who preach
Inciting fear and hatred for their own agenda
Using propaganda
To turn a good man bad

I fight for those who have been imprisoned
For those who have been silenced
Don't allow a minority to speak for the majority
Remember the lessons we learnt from history
Don't allow a repetition of Hitler's war

No race or religion has superiority
No media or government has the authority
To cause divisiveness for their own popularity
To justify the reasons for enforcing austerity
Tactically playing divide and rule to conquer

Perhaps I am misguided
I call it optimistic
But I hope one day to see justice
For those who have faced injustice
By men in suits
Who believe their education makes them astute
Targeting groups to create dispute
Literally playing with human lives
As if they were the creator
Playing at being God

Asma Khatun

Oskar

One day you climb up the scaffolding of a water tower with Oskar. From there you can see from his home's walled compound across to walls
'Look,' says Oskar. Goldie, your huge yellow Labrador, runs across your compound, gaining speed. She reaches the wall and clears it. You've never seen her do this before. You didn't know that she could.
You understand: she's a bush dog, almost wild. With Oskar you watch Goldie sprint up the road between the compounds, into the bush, and she's gone.
Oskar's hair curls, but not so tightly as yours does when it's released from corn rows. He's about the same size as you so maybe about the same age. You've never discussed it, as you didn't discuss climbing the water tower. You both agreed without words. You know you're the same person, best friends, a boy-girl-boy-girl. Although his shorts are more practical than your cotton sun dress, and his eyes are the grey of Russian skies. Your eyes contain facets of an English summer, green and yellow.
At the old house vultures range themselves along the roof, waiting. Around the back, our garden of sprouted beans is dying. You can't see your parents and, when not looking directly at them, their faces aren't describable.
In the distance car drives in silence. As one single body of scraped tawny honey skin you and Oskar descend the water tower. Eventually, and not without mewls of panic, you touch the ground.

Arike Oke

No Rendezvous . . .

As you lean against that ice cold wall
With the tip of your nose pointed at me
The chill is making me shiver
Your ogling eyes are looking glazed
And your smirk is becoming furtive
Mmmh, I can hear you thinking
With your right foot against that wall
Your right hand rubbing your left arm
I am the door and you're the frame
With a hinge, I am drawn.
Silky, your touch so soft
It keeps running down from my lips
Our eyes lock as our fingers intertwine
My heart is like a basketball dribbling
Eyes leaking like an open tap,
As the steam on my lenses condenses
My mouth is an old gutter spilling
You can see the air I expel
You can feel the breath I suck
Smokey, it seems as sweat drops evaporate
Nuzzling my surface for hot spots
A pinch, a poke, a sniff and a squeeze
We're like little kids in a sweet shop
Shades of love shoved into our hearts
Wanting to taste a bit of everything
Beaches, volcanoes, palm tree leaves
This is just a lunchtime treat
Shouts and creams propelled at the sky
No hiding, time wasting or need to fly
That's the climate of the dating scene
No three-date rule to crown a king and queen
A lick, a bite, a nibble, a grind
Our senses become tied up!
As you sweep me off the ground
Our memories are wiped away
So you take me to that place
Where only you and I shall play.

Anisa Abdulrahman

A Loss Less Ordinary

White – the ceiling, the sheets, the grip-crumpled envelope . . . the nurse's
uniform . . . the folder marked 'Jane Doe – amnesiac'.
'Miss? . . . Do you know what was in the syringe you were found with?'
Black.

In the envelope is sheet music, its lipstick-scrawled title 'Room 316'.

316 is a visitors' lounge . . . with a piano.
Everything is an aching blankness, but she can play.
The plaintive notes bring a woman – curvy, young, an expensive-looking suit,
diamond ring.
Her clipboard drops, clattering, her face as pale as autumn mist.
Ms Doe stops playing.
'Do I . . . know you?'

Misshapen lumps of memory tease her like prizes in a Lucky Dip.
Ms Curvy turns her to a wall mirror.
Two identical wide-eyed faces stare back.
Emotions spew into Doe's stomach – a violent mess of recognition.
Temping at the Alzheimer's charity . . .
The sleazy pharmaceutical rep who'd found a cure!
But no, it was . . . wrong?

The room is swaying . . . Her sister's grip tightens.

Her sister's office . . . it's right next door . . . Play Debussy for Sunset ward?
. . .
The rep had flirted – did she have a twin?
The rep was . . . Giles . . .
Giles' files! – He'd dropped one – a top-secret one!
He'd snatched it, she'd seen it –
The cure needed twins – sacrifice one to harvest a cure!

'Giles . . . is *dangerous!*'
'Giles is *mine!* You were Mum's favourite, but I'm *his!*
Well, here's altruism, Miss Lighthouse – arse, you're going to save thousands.'

Lips pursed, phone to her ear.
'Giles? I found her! Bring a stronger dose this time!'

Taria Karillion

My Special Poem

It was May 2012 when I composed a poem for Her Majesty the Queen
To celebrate her Diamond Jubilee
I wrote the poem inside a card
And sent it with congratulations from me

About a week later the postman called
And to my delight and surprise
I saw a letter addressed to me from Buckingham Palace
I could hardly believe my eyes

The letter was from one of Her Majesty's Ladies-in-Waiting
Thanking me on behalf of the Queen
For my message, card and the poem I had composed
To commemorate the Diamond Jubilee

Included with the letter was a pamphlet
With photographs of Her Majesty through the years
I felt so honoured to receive these items
And could not help but shed a few tears

The letter and pamphlet will eventually belong to my granddaughters
And they will treasure them I know
And who knows, perhaps a hundred years down the line
These items may feature on an Antiques Roadshow

I often read my royal letter
And look at the photographs which I hold dear
I am so glad I composed my special poem
To commemorate that historic year.

Jackie Richardson

My Depression

Devoid of logic, absent of sense,
I crave for vision, lest sit on the fence,
To complete a life consumed by doubt,
As I can't really understand
What life is all about.

Triumphantly I rise each day,
Only to find my world has slipped away,
To languish in some uncharted waste,
With no hope of returning in the slightest haste.

Chris Norton

Song Of The Heart

My heart is a powerful yet fragile thing,
because of you this beating, living soul of me can sing,
the flame within still leaps and dances bright.
I can yet know again joy, love and sorrow,
because of you I have a tomorrow.
For you, my angels with smiling faces and kind eyes,
because of you all dark clouds have vanished from glowering skies,
because of you my heart beats,
I live,
because of you.

Paul Andrew Jones

Average Joe

Dull-eyed and sleep deprived
I rise again out of my pit and into the shit that awaits me
I daren't pull back the curtain
That light can be awfully strong this time of day
And plus, I don't want my face to be completely visible yet
Let me just pretend I am somebody else for a while
As if this day is going to be faultless
I can be your average Joe
Wife and kids
9 to 5 in the office
Smiling – for real
Where the blood in my veins doesn't boil like punk music
Instead it saunters down his arms like an old jazz record
Yeah, maybe I'll be him today
Average Joe and his sauntering jazz arms
With his wife whom he probably still loves but doesn't ever make love to
And the kids who may grow old to resent him
But he is happy – or at least was happy for a while
He didn't think about fights and blood and booze and drugs
And what he would have wrote on his suicide note
He just *did* life. As it were meant to be done
With his sauntering jazz arms and his cheating wife
This my friend, is just the average life.

Zak Parsons

Half-Past March

There's a bite to the air but it's fresh and so clean
and the larch down the lane is beginning to green.
There's some daffodils silently trumpeting yellowness
standing serene in rich, earthy mellowness.
The trilling of skylarks and woodpeckers drumming,
melodious sparrows and bumblebees humming,
crows spinning in circles way up above
and the rhythmic lament of a lone collared dove.

Tall mighty oaks, the last trees to green,
dormant, but oozing power and keen -
to show off bare limbs, defiant and proud,
it's almost as if they're boasting out loud.
Male orange-tip butterflies flash tangerine
and female brimstones – the palest of green,
mouth-watering colours and exquisite grace,
spring is now showing her delicate face.

There are clumps of dead-nettles sporting pink hoods
and a scattering of primroses brightening the woods.
Fat catkins exploding on sweet-scented willows
and ladybirds browsing the gold-coloured pillows.
Small larvae are stirring in brown sleeping bags
as the country casts off its drab winter rags.

Janet Vernon

On Sheringham Park

Repton's final volume

I:
We can press far into the ancient core of this land,
searching for things that others might have missed
or passed over in torpid silence;
things that were here long before any of us
and which will remain long after we have gone.

A storm, we are told, might awaken such uncharted worlds,
and so we wait for the cold, for the blackness of rain,
for the deep ragged bass drum of thunder
and for the clean bites of lightning on our eyelids.

Opening our doors to these spirits by night,
the wet breeze smells of autumn and rust
while the apple trees creak in their thick ivy drapes.

The faint concrete streets echo with noise
and gradually fade into parkland and wood.

Under branches, by moss-covered springs,
the stirrings and whisperings of this night
grow stronger;
the sky howls with static and green
as reductionism fails us
and we realise that this place is foreign
in everything from taste to causality.

Hills are Nordic barrows in this world
and their paths serpentine labyrinths
that lead us further into shrouded trees
which glow with the phantom energy
of this storm.

We travel for what feels like centuries,
becoming detached from the towns we left,
clogging up our shoes with rainwater and mud.
Slowly we forget our Westerners' time
and feel the coursing life of this world,
its raw, incomprehensible space
turning before us,
its secrets laid out

in a faculty unknown to language.

II:
We therefore find what we had sought
and as we leave the woodland, the storm
dies and the dawn burns through the cloud belt,
and we return to our towns, unable to speak
of the mysteries that we have seen in the park.

Will Moorfoot

Nefarious Nature

Quickly can a 'pillar spread its wings, the trees shake off their leaves,
the magpie snatches youthful birds for which the mother grieves.
Suddenly the little bird sings, the clouds withdraw their rain,
happy youth time memories lost, the dependent flowers slain.
Rapidly the superfluous sun snatches its wholesome rays,
the kingfisher has been deceived, the prophet left betrayed.

How can the skylark sing his song when others' ears are mute?
Reluctance to the danger, his name in disrepute.
Desperately the flowers yearn for moisture, a hint of cleansing spray,
sullen, dismal and disheartened, they dream of better days.
Hurriedly the sparrows search for branches, far from home they've strayed,
assistance does not find them, by their friends they've been betrayed.

Altruistic is the mother's task that when her job is done,
her offspring take flight and fade into the sun,
What cause is there for laughter when the young ones do depart?
The dove's soulmate slaughtered, ordained for a broken heart.
Rapid is others' growth, the butterfly blooms from its cocoon,
the juvenile caterpillars left, confined to eerie gloom.

Charlotte Rhodes

101

A Victorian Day

Birds' songs drifting,
through heavy curtains.
Servants busily hurrying,
the master's voice to obey.
Brass name plates polished,
steps scrubbed so clean.
Street lights put out,
at the first break of day.

Milk churns clanking,
horses loudly trotting.
Smoking, belching chimneys,
factories throbbing away.
Groaning horse-carts
and trundling trams.
Grumble and trundle,
up the cobbled highway.

Feet swiftly fleeting,
wheelbarrows creaking.
Uniformed peelers dealing,
with crimes of the day.
Organ grinders stalling,
fishmongers calling.
Urchin boys' pleading voices,
barrows of fruit on display.

Oil lamps' glimmering lights,
brazier coke fire sights.
Sparkly rings, pretty things,
amongst haberdashery display.
Shoppers in freedom gaze,
barrow sellers' voices raise.
Fragrant roses and posies,
help in enthralling the day.

Baked potatoes and chestnuts,
battered fish and chip meals.
Whelks, cockles and mussels
and fresh jellied eels.
Exciting bustling scenes,
in jovial Victorian way.
Welcomed my grandparents,
on a busy market day.

Joyce Dawn Willis

Cash

I step out of the office building onto the dark, wet, busy street. Traffic at a standstill, shoppers and workers bustling along, struggling to get home. I am trying to hurry but people are jostling me. It's not easy to hurry. The pavement is wet and these heels are too high!

All the ATMs appear to be in use. I turn the corner and this street seems a little quieter. Not so many people down here. I see an ATM. Great. No one is using it. I struggle in my bag to find my card. I pop it in the machine and enter my pin. I hear a noise behind me. I turn and see a hooded youth close behind. Immediately I begin to get nervous. I begin to get palpitations. Oh please hurry with my cash so that I can move.

At last! I grab my cash and card and shove them in my bag whilst moving as quickly as I can. I take a few steps and I hear the youth shout. I hurry on, faster, faster, faster. I hear hurrying footsteps behind me. I try to run. Awkward in these shoes. I keep going, aware of him running and shouting behind me. Suddenly my ankle twists, my heel snaps and I go down with a *thud!* I try to get up. I see the youth standing over me. I let out a terrified scream. But then I see what he is holding out towards me – my debit card!

Anne Williams

Poppies For Remembrance

In fields of Flanders deep in France
The breeze makes them bob, sway, dance.
Weather-hardy poppy, flower petals of blood red
Black velveteen centre, national symbol for our forces dead.

Eleventh month, eleventh hour, eleventh day
We praise actions of our brave fallen
Tragedy for public sobbing
Grief of families in mourning
War, conflict, join together present and past
Haunting tune of bugler as he plays to the silent at last.

Thousands of heads held low, a mark of respect
Lost deep in thought, a tide of sadness was wept
Tortured heroic souls
Who died for peace
Hopeful sacrifice would ensure fighting would cease.

Reminder lest we never forget
Honour our noble hearts, learn the fates they met
Elderly veterans, medals pinned high on breast
Marching salute to fallen comrades
Fist beats upon their chest.

Bravely recalled on Armistice Day
They fight for every one of us
Come home safe we worry and pray.

Jackie Smith

Quarry Wood Revisited

A dark wind steals through stricken trees where we once stood.
Low, leaden skies, which once had burned so blue.
Sun-spangled waters, dulled to Winter's sullen flood,
And I'm alone here, lost in thoughts of you.

Of yesterday, when Love was wild, was sweet.
Deep in our secret world among the pine
We watched the Wind; Succumbed to Summer's heat.
You swore you loved me, kissed me; You were mine.

We smiled our secret smiles, we dreamed our dreams.
You breathed my name . . . Maybe we loved too well.
Our stolen moments slipped away so soon, it seems
Fate, in its jealousy, destroyed the spell.

Our Summer's gone. This wood's a silent place
Where, like your love, the Pines began to die.
Fire turned to ice: Indifference chilled your face.
Dreams palled to dross beneath a mocking sky.

Now our eyes meet, then fall away.
Just strangers now. Blind pity's all I see.
So we pass by. The darkening shadows twine too high
Around my soul, to let you back to me.

But ghost winds haunt these stricken trees
To raise dead leaves . . . dead memories.

D. S.

If This Is Heaven

If this is Heaven,
note those cloaked in dirt,
or scabbed and bloody
in a punctured shirt,

lying dying on the dirt of a
stained-grey road
as passers-by pass by wishing
cameras to load

and upload the sight to
a dozen or so likes,
seeing as lungs lose breath
and a life quickly dies.

If this is Heaven,
flick a switch and watch old news,
see repeated new instances of
the violence of views

that condone killing children
and planting bombs in schools,
where Samaritans lose their heads
because it's violence that rules,

speaking loudly with its voice built
on hate and hate and hate
with which compassionate minds shall
not negotiate.

If this is Heaven,
drink its nectar in binge
or facilitate its message
with brick-dust and syringe

that mottles red veins into
yellow-blue bruises
and become the used
like each that uses,

until they are found out or
the time when they are caught
between four walls, barred windows,
where life is retaught.

If this is Heaven,
Pandora's box spat out cancer,
with AIDS and Ebola and
little hope of an answer

to the ignominy and pain
of a prolonged death
that rattles on and rattles on
in the weakest of breaths,

knowing only time is able
of restoring lost pride,
in delivery of the end
from which none can hide.

If this is Heaven,
value paper more than people,
For though neither can proclaim
To be the route of every evil,

neither can survive
without existence of the other as
each is both the keeper
and the murderous brother.

If this is Heaven,
God is a green-printed face;
if this is Heaven,
it's a Hell of a place.

Jack Desambrois

All Of The Lights

You are all of the lights in my life.

You light up my life,
Like the sun lights up the sky in summertime,
You bring me so much warmth and happiness,
I feel I have more hope and strength in your brightness.

You light up my life,
Like the moon lights up the night,
Here in the dark,
You are my guiding star,
And I feel so safe lying in your arms,
There is nowhere I'd rather be,
Than right here with you holding me.

You are all of the lights in my life,
Like . . .
The sparkling fireworks on Bonfire Night,
The thousands of candles lit worldwide at Diwali time,
The coal burning in the fire on a cold winter's night.

You are all of the lights in my life,
Like . . .
The road signs, streetlights and traffic lights guiding me in the right direction,
The tunnel lights steering me back on course to my next destination,
The spotlights showering me with affection and attention.

You are all of the lights in my life,
Like . . .
The flashlights, headlights, strobe lights,
The floodlights that come on when the rain pours down,
The lightning to my thunder,
The lighthouse beacon that keeps me away from the storm,
And saves me from going under.

You are all of the lights in my life,
Like . . .
The floating Chinese lanterns, the soft glow of candlelight, the beautiful
Northern Lights,
The colourful, pretty Christmas tree lights,
The stunning sparkle of the diamond ring you put on my finger last night.

Glimmering, glistening, glittering,
Shining, shimmering, scintillating,

From day to night,
You are all of the lights in my life.

In my world, you are the most important, sacred light,
You are the love of my life.

Amee Shah

In Death

Seldom do you see their fragile bodies lie.
Only to simply disappear without trace.
For the many millions, no reminder of their time here on Earth -
and no final resting place.

Except for little homestead or dwelling place, in perhaps tree or hedgerow can
be found.
And their offspring give any clue as to a life once had.
For these glorious creatures are a miracle of nature -
and for their short lives alongside us we should be glad.

For they bring joy to so many.
To be awakened by dawn chorus, or to watch them soaring so effortlessly high
in the sky.
To see them bravely take to the white waters of a cruel sea -
or visiting urban back garden as you sit and watch time go by.

As they so gracefully skim the surface of a gently flowing river
And whose song fills the air with perfect melody.
Whose daily ever presence seems to brighten even the gloomiest of days.
To gladden the heart – they are nature's remedy.

Much a life lived in secrecy -
and there too in death, perhaps them we are not meant to find.
But if we were to lose them all, what a bleak world in which we would live -
and surely would mark the beginning of the end for mankind.

James Allen

The Grey Room

We are programmed
by society,
our families,
and genes.

I am stuck in limbo
between pursuing a dream
and listening to
the silent echoes
of ancient stimuli.

How do I switch it off?

If I were to be reborn
I would make the same
mistakes again,
but I would also enjoy
the same successes.

How can I cleanse myself
of the programmed thinking
that freezes me
in my attempts to
honestly create,
to fulfil my dreams,
my passions.

If I create
a perfect environment
without obstructions
or distractions
to my creative process
regardless of its chaos,
being surrounded
by beauty
or minimalism.

If I locked myself
into a grey room -
would I be able to

get the flow,
to reach that high,
to use my full potential
to paint
the next masterpiece?

What if?

Eva J K Skarviken

The Woods

Cautiously I crept through the crimson, auburn foliage. Autumn leaves gently crunching beneath my aching, throbbing feet. Unforgiving thorns tugged at my trousers as I scrambled ever deeper into the dense woodland. Ancient oaks engulfed me, whispering to each other as I passed them. Biting winds whipped between the withering trunks of the old oaks, howling loudly and angrily, battering my bare arms. Gazing up towards the decaying branches, arched precariously over me, I could see the grimacing grey clouds gathering above. *Splash!* A tiny drop of rain landed on my cheek then another and another, before I knew it the rain was pounding hard through the canopy of leaves and striking my skin like darts. I knew I needed to find shelter. Shelter? Where? The rain fell harder, faster. I had to keep moving. I could hear a rumbling in the distance, a raging, ravenous roar of thunder heading for me. Searching for me. I needed to hide, find refuge, safety. Carefully I started jogging through the mossy, damp carpet that lay before me, my legs weary and heavy. I needed to keep going. Find shelter. Be safe. Relentlessly the icy rain still pounded, my previously white vest now smeared with dirt and blood and clinging to my cold, drenched torso. Onward I rambled. Virtually blinded by the piercing rain. Suddenly... *thud!* A twisted root grabbed me. My head hit the ground. It was hazy now but in the distance I saw the edge of the wood. So close.

Miriam Bartley

Office Frogger . . . An Ode To My Frogging Friend!

My frogging friend plays with such style and grace
He gives nothing away with the look on his face
His game is quiet, he makes no noise
There is a certain skill, a knack, such poise!
He lands it every time squarely on the mat
But I've a secret weapon that will knock him flat
I'll put sugar in his coffee when he looks away
That's sure to put him off his winning way!
With slight of hand and twist of newt
I'm sure to win a game at last, you beaut!
But . . . wait! I couldn't really do that to my frogging friend
Cos I wouldn't ever never want our friendship to end!

Jane Dowson

Jeeps

Firebird sweeps past
Revolution in motion
Inspiration stems at first sight
At the bus stop
Whizzing by the
Army jeep
Swapped by a red Jeep, *beep, beep*
Spies abroad our invasion
Walk
Alongside the roadside
Jeeps in tandem
One after the other
Inspires us
To go on . . .
To the end of the road.

S M Thompson

Pour Me Some Flowers Please

Would you like a cup of gypsophilia
Or maybe a rose of sky blue?
There are some sumptuous lilies
That you might like a splash of, or two;
A couple of clusters of chrysanthemums
All sparkling in lemons and creams;
For your taste buds' delight and to make
It just right, how about a scattering
Of sweet peas in delicate hues?
From a gleaming snow-white teapot
Served in fluted vessels so fine,
Drinking this nectar fills you with vigour
A taste experience utterly divine:
These are all found in abundance
By the train tracks that slide
Alongside the wild fields;
Rustled by the winds, sprinkled with sand,
This Yorkshire paradise is sure to appeal.

Pour me some flowers please . . .

Angela Gloker

Letters Of Him

D, – How he always keeps his dignity.
A, – And always loves me.
V, – He never has vanity, he just looks at me.
 I, – And he says, 'I, love you too' after my, 'I, love you!'
D, – Don't say goodbye in a letter because the words about you are true and I,
     will like you will always love you like you love me too!.

Annabelle Claire

Angels

Heavenly light shine from above
surround me with your endless love,
there's evil all around me,
keep back my enemies
who would crawl under my skin
and feed upon the flesh within.
Keep away the darkness
that they feed upon,
that's why I need your support and love
to help me carry on.

Angels beside me,
angels above me,
angels take care of me
and my family.

Don't let my prayers wither and die,
give me strength to overcome
for every day I look to you, to get me through
the long hours and endless days.
I need your support and love
I'm weak, not strong
I need you beside me
to help me carry on.

Angels beside me,
Angels above me,
Angels take care of me
And my family.

Sandra Wood

Life's Will

'Why am I here?'
The robin sweetly sang
'Why am I here?'
Alone he felt a pang
'Where is my dear?'
He looked all around him
The sky was now clear
And yet he still sat there
Staring at trees now bare
Perched on that sill
Not knowing why
Yet knowing it was life's will
He came every day
Watching the sky fall away
And every day he heard desperate cries
Coming from the window
Tears rolling from black eyes
Shaking, the lady had come to her tether
Tired of being alive, tired of the cold weather
For the first time in a month she looked through her window
Hearing sweet chirping melting her sorrow
A smile played at the end of her lips
As a robin stroked his legs against her fingertips
Everything was going to be alright
She sighed
Death was always nearby
But all around her there was life.

Charleen Powell

Through The Wood She Goes

Through the wood she goes
On a sumptuous summer's day,
Her footsteps falling
With silent grace,
Her skirt billowing softly
In the breeze.

The sunshine beams and the mercury rises
On this sumptuous summer's day,
The trees alive
With heavenly birdsong,
The flowers bowing, carpeting
Her unspoken path.

A dormouse scurries, an owl swoops
This sumptuous summer's day,
Her midnight locks
Trailing elegantly behind,
Her warm coffee eyes
Focusing vacantly ahead.

Weather changes as she goes
On her sumptuous summer's day,
The wind rushing
Through the trees,
The butterflies still dancing
Beautifully above her.

A wolf howls a warning
On our sumptuous summer's day,
Her shawl tightening
Shielding from harm,
Her pace gaining haste
To reach safety.

Through the wood she goes on,
What was a sumptuous summer's day,
The sky now black
(More so than night)
Our young girl runs
And falls.

But she's not afraid,
She lives here now
Her old life far away,
She knows in the wood she's not alone
And yet here it is she'll stay.

Roya Alsopp

Cornish Fantasy

A tiny old world fishing village, quaint and picturesque
With little whitewashed cottages, that rise up on the crest
Cobbled streets that twist and turn the ancient harbour wall
Where nets are drying, sea birds crying and the wild waves call

Pretty painted window boxes, gaily coloured doors -
Bid you welcome as you climb up from the rocky shores.
Old stone inns that stood the years and heard the smugglers' tales
Of buried treasure, shipwrecked clippers and the stormy gales.

The fishing vessels in the harbour, weighing out the catch,
The old church quiet and peaceful, as you lift the ancient latch.
Gift shops in the High Street, where we spent such happy hours
A teashop with its dainty china – bowls of fragrant flowers.

Out from the restless heights, the watchful eyes forever gaze
The figurehead from some old prow – a glimpse of bygone days
King Arthur's sceptred realms of peerless knights with courage bold
The golden age of chivalry, deep woven in the mould

The rugged caves where one is said to hear the mermaids sing
The ruined castle on the cliff top and the piskies' ring
The legends of the Druids and the lonely moor land ways
The gardens, hills and headlands of the lovely Cornish bays.

Beryl Shepard Leece

Love Language

I love language
Got an affection for inflection
A passion for captions
An obsession for inflection
Pronouns
Proverbs
Adjectives
Adverbs
Abstracts in essays
It's absolutely absurd
How I'm cuddling commas and double entendres
I hold on to colons so long
My muscles are stronger
I long for a couple of genres
Fact or fiction
Distinguish my English
My diction is different
Listen
If Bad Boy 'Invented The Remix'
I'll reverse a word so it ends in a prefix
Forget letter bombs
Each letter's a bomb
The powerful blast of paragraphs is extra strong
The MC's MC Escher
Etch an image with the lexicon
To go a step beyond the competitors
To the upper echelons
If you're down art's cathartic
Now the pressure's gone
Released through speech
Now I know why the caged bird tweets
With improper grammar
I see through gloss and glamour
Drop the hottest stanzas
Till doctors at Stanford adopt the standard
My dissertations for different nations

If they're Caucasians, Cajuns
Or came from the Caymans
My cadence caters to any occasion
This creativity can't be caged in
The margins of pages
Phrases cascading
Escaping from A4
Brainstorms raining
My thoughts gush
In the form of a chorus
My corpus discussed before the caucus
Course bruv
I call the bluff of frauds that talk tough
Better be cautious
Keep your jaws shut
I eat a dictionary
And swallow a thesaurus
Walls covered in more books
That's how I was brought up
Hooked from a young age before Wikipedia
It was the Britannica Children's Encyclopedia
T-rexes
Romans
Robots
Meteors
Then I got greedier
Craved something meatier
Not greasier just easier to digest
My dialect's food for thought
Coming live and direct
Don't digress
Stay on point like quills and cursors
My cursive surfs surfaces without curses, sir
Panoramic language captures the Earth's curvature
Their rhetoric's repetitive
Logic just circular
No surplus verbs

Each word is perfect
Were it written for the right purpose
If not
It's worthless
I love language

Call me The Wordsmith

Tommy Evans

Summer Spectacle

It has arrived, the summer I have waited for,
Clocks have been adjusted, and so we awake
To lighter mornings and evening sunshine.
The housework must be left, I am so fortunate
To live by the sea.
Off I go, walking along the prom,
Sometimes a stroll on the beach, tide permitting
Kick off my sandals and enjoy a paddle,
The children's shrieks of laughter, music to my ears.
A seat in the sun, must dry feet,
Then home for a cuppa.
This to me is summer, no crowded trains or busy airports,
Just enjoying nature and happy faces
These days will be remembered when winter arrives
Although I can sit by a fire with a riveting book
The down side being I'll have to dust again!
So I will enjoy this lovely summer season,
Give thanks I am still able, old age has crept up
But hey, no worries, the sun is still shining,
God is in His Heaven, thank you summer
For making an old lady very happy, a spectacle indeed.

Freda Symonds

Non-Church

Do you take thee, transcended devotee
to be thy unlawful of all in store?
Will thou blindfold mundane tranquillity
whilst violently richer or for poor?
It's out with pews and in with sterile floor
sedated glowing labyrinth of aisles,
promise will thou love as an open door
and hunt addiction down in single file?
We'll queue until we're coughing only bile
believing deficit we can't manage,
but every penny helps when in denial
accepting of collateral damage.
So cherish all until an early hearse,
come worship in the temple of commerce.

David Dixon

Thin And Broken

The last time I saw you, you were thin and broken. I had seen you like that
before though, just less close to death. Four summers before you decided
to take up yoga and quit drinking beer. And, while this was all to mask the
unbearable pit of depression you found yourself in, it suited you.
But now, disorientated from the medication and tired of saying goodbye, it
was different. I talked aimlessly for an hour to make myself feel better, to make
you all feel better. I talked aimlessly to try and cover the elephant in the room,
your unavoidable and desperate desire to be gone.
As I left I whispered, 'You've got to be strong and fight,' because that's what
you say to dying people, isn't it? I knew you wouldn't though. I knew you
couldn't. A week later you were gone.
Two weeks after that we buried you, thin and broken.

Lauren Stevenson

Because My Child

There you rest your eyes
I'll never let those
Innocent views die
Because my child
I will protect you.

There you reach for protection
From those external hardships
But you'll never lack affection.
Because my child
I will protect you.

There you grasp my finger,
I'm comfort, just keep hope
That this moment will linger
Because my child
I will protect you.

There you go my baby, crawl away
Reach your hopes, do not worry
Here is where I'll stay
Because my child
I will protect you.

There you take those little steps
I'll help you reach the heights
Where your dreams are kept
Because my child
I will protect you.

There you go for you wander so far
For now my child, just
Wish upon, upon a star
Because my child
I will protect you.

Amy Herbert

Mystic Autumn

Summer's fading, mystic autumn nears,
Goldfinches perch on gossamer thistledown
Swifts and swallows all are long since gone,
And leaves are turning yellow, red and brown.

Buzzard flies high in the westering sky
Towards the sunset, red as fire;
The sweet fresh air off the distant moor
Turns colder, fresher, and smells of autumn mire.

Dry, rustling leaves crunch underfoot,
Crackle and snap in the road, in the lane;
Squirrel gathers nuts to hoard for winter,
And sweet-smelling gorse flowers once again.

One early morning a vee of geese fly high,
Winging north again to colder climes,
To pastures new, as all migrating birds,
And will return again in warmer times.

Misty, sometimes foggy autumn morns,
Rooks cawing loudly in trees bereft of leaves,
Trunks gilded silver by some early frosts,
Stand, waiting for winter's first big freeze.

Now cold, impenetrable fogs are closing in
And swirling mists flow over boggy moor
The autumnal darkening day grows shorter still -
All life is slowing down to await the thaw.

Is it the ancient Celtic pagan myths
That draw me now to seasons' rhythmic span,
When time was measured by falling leaves, or green,
And all was honoured and revered by ancient Man?

Diana Price

Justice Quest

Visible there was the lone still figure
Stopping to catch breath, walking 'cross the moor,
Solitary, surrounded by bleakness
But happy within Nature's wilderness.
Surveying the terrain that lay around,
The wind very nearly the only sound;
He saw in the distance a high peak rise,
Hearing occasional bird cries.
His mouth getting drier, he felt so wear
But he could see no sign of water near;
Feeling regret he earlier forsook
To fill his flask from a refreshing brook.
Growing 'cross the sky, a mass of dark cloud
Loomed, threatening in its arrogance proud
To unleash a vast watery torrent
For sake of some unknown grievance to vent.
The arrogance with which it threatened him
Matched that of those men, whom upon a whim
Had forced him to this point; now an outcast,
Because he knew great secrets from their past.
As upon his knees, to the ground he fell
Sprawling, his hand touched the edge of a well;
Filling his flask, beginning to drink,
Noticing the sun beginning to sink,
He decided to settle for the night.
Extinguishing his lamp, in the moonlight
He bathed, finally falling into sleep;
Lucid was his slumber, enchanting, deep.
Waking up with a start to a changed view,
With the feeling of his dream coming true
He found himself near his destination,
Boosting morale to complete his mission
To see those men punished for making threats,
It was time he revealed their secrets
Of corrupt cruelty, to local press.
Exposed for their desire to oppress
Local folk; the subjects took their power
Away, sending them off to the Tower –
A hideous and isolated place,

A confining future for them to face.
For his knowledge they would not let him be,
Life in prison for them, and he lived free;
A man too honest for their bribery,
And well attuned to Nature's mystery.

Michael Vickery

Ainsdale – North Of Liverpool Bay

The golden grains of sand hold together hand-in-hand
To give the sand dunes
Winds blow across them, singing their tunes
The starfish on the seabed
Silently glide and hide in their world
The waves gently flow to and fro
The moonlight creeps around
The frogs make their sound
For this is the beach at Ainsdale
It's seen many a gale
The weather can be tough, the sea can be rough
A wreck lies here
History unfolds, stories told
It hides beneath the sands
It came from American lands
The Star of Hope, an ocean liner
From Wilmington, North Carolina
Appearing like a ghost
When the tide is out along this Liverpool coast
All the crew were rescued long ago
Mysteries hidden here and buried
Some we will never know.

Isabel Taylor

An Evening With A Dancing Spirit

I'll give you one now, all for free
since base 'twould be to charge a fee:

'A man, like mirrors, presents one image
of multiple shades when the sun is out,
but if light removed and darkened without,
then those same colours lose life and diminish.'

Ah, how much is lost in shadows,
all form and no matter!
Well, is there one who knows
how to free us of this problem latter?

Volume announces the fool,
so here I go,
'tis me you know!
Let's skim the top of my wisdom pool:

'Even in base surroundings
one may still hold noble bearings;
like the sun alone in darkness
still warmly shines regardless . . .'

Ah but wait, that's two I've now given you!
Though perhaps you'll argue (and goodly too!)
that I merely diagnosed half of wrong,
and cured with half of healthy song!

You wish my mouth to move some more?
Either you tease or wish to please.
I should really be silent, else I'll bore,
for all know wisdom o'erflows into follies.

But life is indeed short,
and I so do love to retort!
Well here goes, your patience will be tested,
but then your minds are usually so well rested!

Though before I get comfortable,
let me address that creature over there,
huddled alone with cold and hated stare,
dreaming a vainly self-aimed fable:

'To the sullen rock near yonder:
is thy small misery such wonder?

Let sweet music and joy resound,
remove thy brow's encumb'ring frown.'

'No man is so great that he can't
wish the happiness of others.
Be as gentle to others
as you are harsh to yourself!'

I reckon his care is the reverse
of this fair and goodly verse!

Ah, why waste words on the deaf!
As silent fall my well-meant notes
I'll leave him to his living death;
instead I'll give my friends my quotes.

Come, I've a tale to tell,
who knows what wisdom shall spring
from out of this deeply well;
gather round and listen in.

Thus, as sight turns from darkness to light,
so my thoughts turn to love – all men's right.

But my good friends I hope you'll spare me
the sadness encumbered in my mem'ries,
and allow me to instead of myself
tell of a young man named Welf:

A tall and handsome man was he,
lately returned from travelling the seas;
quick and sharp of eye,
'twas not long before he spied
fair Pelopia for his bride.

Of all his great qualities
there was in lesser measure,
but equal in potency,
flaws to spoil his treasures.

Common 'tis to most men,
but not common in him,
as full to the brim
was his fear of women.

So himself he hid
and blamed on inclination

that which would call him timid,
and in love gave himself starvation.

Fair Pelopia in this did not share,
for she was lively in her fare,
and drinking deep the skies above
soon became drenched in love.

But do not blame Welf too hard,
for conversation he had tried,
though for fear all thoughts were barred;
thus for him she threw all thoughts of love aside.

In darkness he found himself,
for seeing the sun behind her eyes
could not see past her to the open skies.
Thus, one night came to dreaming Welf:

Her sweet illusory face,
which keeps him warm
as he embraces empty space.
Will nothing calm his inward storm?

Awakes doth he
and shouts loudly:

'O phantom, wilt thou give me peace,
or further torment me with the vision of a kiss?
And wilt these phantom kisses cease,
or let me languish in imagined bliss?!'

To silence doth his anger rage,
no beast has he to wound or cage.
And anger long repressed
soon turns on him depressed.

'Together we flew and scorched the night sky,
burning brilliant we forced the sun to rise!
But really I am here alone and cold,
cursed to spend the night with naught to hold.'

'Many have I seen within my dreams,
but you call to me as my waking need.
And nothing compares to dearest P.
for shadows they are to thee.'

'Though dreams are but water and bread
to love, they are all that save my head!
And in these, though you be free and wholly thine,
I can still lay claim to thy beauty as mine.'

'Ah, the sun with easterly winds rises,
so now too must I reapply my disguises.
Must I daily wrench my soul from out the well,
to dry it off and make presentable?'

Here see what becomes of ill health
mixed unreservedly with time as wealth.
What is hell but the silence that creeps
into men's ears when alone in darkness deep.

Ah, but this sad story
wrenches my throat to tell,
I'll cut short and skip o'er hell,
and leave you of his sorrows free.

Suffice to say,
time runs away.
For what cost?
The girl was lost.

To her, Welf was but a statue grey;
to him, no more shall she light his days.

Forgive me, that melancholy song
I cannot sing for very long.
Though perhaps 'tis best
for friends are meant for jest.

See now, how the moon hovers high
enclosed by stars aloft the sky.
We'd best be gone to bed,
and forget all I've said.

Hopefully tomorrow you'll be better told
by someone of greater wisdom old.
But just before we go,
I'll leave you one last crow:

'One day, for all days, you will die,
but with this knowledge do not cry;
the universe was born with you,
the universe will die with you.

So reunite thy spirit twain,
for 'tis not death, but simply pain!
Until to dust your body be bade,
live well, live long; soon eternal shade.'

John Rupp

Will No Longer

The bride will no longer wear white
The warrior will no longer fight
As the sun replaces the moonlight
And we forget to play our part

The rain will no longer fall
The phone will no longer call
As the short become the tall
And we sacrifice the heart

The earth will no longer bear the storm
The actor will no longer perform
As the soldier refuses to conform
And we learn to breathe again

The living will no longer die
The birds will no longer fly
As the mind forgets to question why
And we let the tears stain

So when the sun no longer shines
And the world appears to be unkind
Just remember these words of mine
And together we will be, for all time.

Graham Connor

Pride's Encumb'ring Hide

Unfurl thy wide and barren soul's sails,
and let arise deep winds of freedom fill
those great wings to ride Nature's fierce gales,
lest tight bonds rub, restrain and make thee ill.
So dance and shake off pride's encumb'ring hide,
thus some sun may reveal Man beneath
the cold and starlit smoke of distant pride.
For though love desires what's secret sheathed,
it first needs know of some matter missing,
else you're taken for whole when but a part.
Why be other than who you are being?
For each feature and value you distort
steals life from brief changing creation,
and robs consciousness from thy sullen mind.
What's gained in guise is but imitation
of the fair beauty for which thou now pines.
So instead let all others speak and see
the truth, and be but a mirror to thee.

William Rupp

Beautiful Women E'er Where I Go

Beautiful women e'er I go
to see thy smiles and thy eyes,
whose tender charms, since all soft lies,
breathe life that steals all my woes.

Give me a maid of kindly heart
who shyness hides, so shineth pride,
though quiet eyes a look confides,
gives life that steals all pain's parts.

Yet ere I go: I dream to know a dove
whose home is charm yet heart is charged with love.

Joseph Rupp

The Ways In Which I Find Myself

My leather bound soliloquy speaking to whomever shall read.
I wake up in the shadow of a dream or, perhaps this time, it's reality mistaken for such.
The freedom of catharsis is buried within my sculpture of words,
The seduction of obsidian ink that bleeds into a cinematic performance on the page.
Memories play as if on a silver screen, the light dancing elegantly on the walls.
Calligraphic trees stand arthritic beneath the violaceous veil of a pastel night;
Much like the candle weeping its twisted hollow, the beads betraying the golden flame
I too melt, into my words.

Gemma Louise Rose

Finished. Done.

Stroll around why don't you?
Take yourself onto the empty canvas.
Dab muddy white, dab the sky blue
Twist and turn your bristles stew –

Messy strokes forming twigs and leaves
Shades of colours fathomless as the sea.
Dusty brown mulled into terracotta trees

Creamy orange seeping with magenta
Your serene strokes forming full of life flowers.
Freeze yourself in ice blue lilies,
Strolling around the deep blue ocean.

Your slithery black splashes stream across the pavement
Forming shadow monsters across the dark slabs
Finally you take one more stroll around
And finally you're finished. Done.

Farah Akram

Up Came A Flower

Up came a flower, so brightly dancing
as it swayed in the gentle breeze.
Golden petals play upon the flowing
wind, lighting all growing life and trees.

A sullen boy picked her up, plucked her petals round,
and threw her crying down to the ground.
In the wind she will live on and spread seeds,
but the boy in sickly lands – buried in weeds.

Geraldine Rupp

The Unlived Day

Come! Leave off those dusty tomes of learning,
in the bosom of the world find thy fate;
fly and soar for what you're truly yearning,
dare you not postpone the much prolonged date!

Don't meekly reckon on some unlived day
of stars in scope too great they lack all warmth,
and forgetfully lose thy life away;
but summon bright your mirth and fast pour forth,
proclaiming to all unending ages
thy passion for life eternal rages!

So striding forth from out the hermit's cave
to brave fate's path, no more to fear: a slave.

Thus, as countless Suns and burning gods
thy spirit aflamed with hot commands
will conquer all fresh impending odds,
and shine a titan in mortal lands!

George Rupp

Memories

Does she remember the touch of my hand,
The dreams we shared,
The first kiss?
Does he remember our drunken stupor,
Our comradery thicker than blood,
The girl we once shared.

I remember all this,
And oh, so much more.

I remember her laugh,
Her wandering eyes,
The love our bodies shared.

I remember his brilliant stubbornness,
His vast, abstract knowledge,
The fights we carried each other through.

I doubt they remember a thing,
But to my pain I remember it all,
And oh, so, so much more.

I remember her cries,
I remember her pain,
I remember watching her leave,
Our time reduced to but a memory.

I remember his punch,
I remember his screams,
I remember the day I became less than dirt,
The day our brotherly bond became but dust in the winds of time.

I remember all this,
And so much more

The memories of joy and laughter a taunting jokester,
Reminding me of what was and will never be again,
A sword that disembodies all hope,
All hope of recovery.

The memories of anguish, of suffering,
Maggots burrowing into my brain,
Breeding in my dreams,
Soiling my name unto myself.

It is this of which my true illness lies,
My one true curse,
One that dwells within the bed I made,
One which robs me of the ability to forget.

I will never forget,
Lest I shall always be forgot.

Jai Small

Justice For Oscar

He got four years. A jail term for a crime.
His doing nothing paid for with this time.
An old man, losing teeth and hair and hearing
Who in his youth assisted in the shearing
The denuding of those endless swarms of victims,
The poor, the dispossessed, unwanted millions.
They each lost life, a child, a family;
His fingers touched their money. Guiltily?
It matters not. He didn't fight to stop
An evil system; orders from the top
Ordained his days, a grubby, cold accounting
Of ordinary folk who fed the mounting
Death toll. He just did his job each day
So very long ago. Old man in grey.
Three hundred thousand lives cut off in hate,
Now justice done, the mills grind slow and late.
But is it truly justice? Weigh the scales!
Three hundred thousand dead – four years in jail
For aiding and abetting, acquiescing.
Somewhere the love of God spreads out, caressing.

Vivien Foster

Nylon Strings

There was a parcel left for me yesterday;
dressed in red ribbon and fancy writing.
I had come back from work
with weary bones, weary mind.
The house was full of dust
it hadn't be tidied for a while.
I took a sigh, turned on the kettle,
and sat down unwrapping the beige paper.
Sitting inside was an old cassette
no note, no name.
With a little hesitation I plugged in my stereo,
put the cassette inside and without another thought
I pressed play.
I closed my eyes as I recognised your honest voice
singin' our truths
along your refreshing beat.
A cold stream of music tickled my ankles
forcing my stuffy surroundings to drip away.
I stepped forward into the ocean
and let my body free-fall onto the surface,
a splash of colour burst as I sunk deep
to a world of water; of the tears I had cried
the laughter I had once sung
all the smiles and the frowns
the warmth and the coldness of my heart
intertwined.
Your lyrical exhibit sang to me,
flooded my surroundings with bright coral
and strange shadows I could not recognise.
I sat still with a lowered head
as I explored and swam on.
The ocean was so vast
though my sorrows hadn't left me
I could no longer cry.
Your essence
the streams of light from the surface
from my life's aquarium
revealed old memories I had forgotten
newer hopes, greater times,

a promise of a world full of everything
as the music faded
I saw a room not full of clutter
but a home.

Stacey Rezvan

Protective

Radiance so pure, innocence so precious and poignant; that's what my baby has. That's what I *must* protect! She says she's ready for the world, but I say she isn't.
My wife said I'm too protective; that I'm killing her, am I? I don't know. I made her snowflake skin, her sapphire eyes, her chestnut hair. They're mine! But, I can't – just can't, bear the thought of another man knowing her.
I won't let anyone else spoil her with their stares, their words or their thoughts. I won't. I'll do whatever it takes to keep her with me, and for me; keep her just my girl, my secret, forever…

***

He won't even let me see the light of day! Father is so, so, *guarded!* I know he loves me, but he is swallowed by worry, and because of that I'm swallowed by him – kept inside. Such is justice! I really don't know if I can stand being trapped any longer though; the deprivation, it's killing me slowly…

***

My wife was *never* wrong. I remember what she once said: 'Amazing, isn't it? Whatever clothes your wear on the outside changes you on the inside.'
Like always she was right. The essence of my nights spent in knickers, bras and cross-dressing in general has diffused through my skin to my very soul. My suppressed femininity is alive but withers every day she is caged. I love her dearly, but no one can ever know! No one will ever know…

Christopher Rayner

Reoffending Visitor

Why did you come when not invited? We sighted you, yes
And in spite of you guess
At what was the cause.

Unplanned but expected, you have us infected
You fanned the flame, and now
You're to blame
For this breakdown in humanity, rise in insanity,
Connections, links
Friendships, courtships
Jinxed
Broken, and spoken about
In gritty, bitter, bin litter language.

You creep into our lives
Like you seep into the very fabric of our carpets.

Carpets heavy with the sorrow that you spilt.
You spilt your sorrow.
Please, tomorrow
You go. Enough.
Your crocodile tears
Increase our fears, and slowly start to drown . . .
Everything.

Whose is that face?! Just an outline, a trace
In that photo . . .
It's floating away from its place,
Now soggy and sodden
Memory forgotten,
Paper drenched, frame rotten.

Just another victim to the uninvited floods. Our floods.
Oh how we claim that ownership.

We own the floods, bemoan the floods.
But so pretty surely, the glimmering, shimmering?
But no, overshadowed by the simmering
Threat

Of more to come. More which when done,
Will aid and abet
And continue to set us
Apart.

Emma Vickery

I Feel . . .

I feel like a tortoise going nowhere at speed,
I feel like a prisoner who'll never be freed.
I feel like an athlete who's last in the race,
I feel like the victim who's in the wrong place.
I feel like a problem that cannot be solved,
I feel like a tablet that's slowly dissolved.
I feel like a candle that's long burned out,
I feel like an ice cube that's started to melt.
I feel like a purse that holds no money,
I feel like a joke that no one finds funny.
I feel like a star that never shines bright,
I feel like a bird that cannot take flight.
I feel like a boat that's destined to sink,
I feel like a pen that's run out of ink.
I feel like an object that's stashed in the loft,
I feel like the chocolate that never got scoffed.
I feel like a ball that's never been kicked,
I feel like an option that nobody picked.
I feel like a human who doesn't belong,
I feel like I'm living a life that's all wrong.

Clare Slater

Stumbled

Satan, you stumbled upon the wrong prey
Hey, how does it feel to be stalked upon?
Weapons and people you placed in our way
May some day turn upon you, Satan
Batons used to beat us with will sponge-up
Sponge-like slippery grips will wither
Whether today or tomorrow they will soften
Soften your grip upon our souls
Souls of your helpers will cry in pain
Pain inflicted upon us for years
Years of cruelty upon cruelty
Will rightly land at your clawed feet
Feats that you administered will lose their standing
Standing us in good stead to defeat your armies
Army of angels have heard our pleas
Please step back, take your place there
There we will stalk you and taunt you
You have no place here so stumble on
On to your next prey

Carmen Hedman

Summer Hours

Poppies blowing in the breeze
Swifts and swallows flying high
The sky so blue, the sun so bright
Warm air brings the hedgehogs out at night
It's lovely to be in the garden
Listening to the birds singing away
Bees busy in the flowers
Making the most of the summer hours.

Anita C Walker

Tenderness

Pining doesn't live here.
A crow-song in the distance,
love came through my window;
a passing breeze, a resting warmth
as my hand closed its arch.
This kitchen: mote embedded, a
scramble of moments, a fury of
crumbles. Two cats
running through. This mind:
furious, scrambled, reaching
for too many

unfinished pens.

Only God speaks in the night;
mingled with sated yearnings
restive conclusions. The hand
content not to reach.

So, what, in the temporal
in the demanding, has space
for love? A hand closes, a
kitchen a-crumble
falls into dust. All stills.
The moat making quiet swirls.

Safe.

Remote.

. . . and far from the growing Sun.

A. Wikman

Number Without Name

Call me thirty plus
Being named with pain
Number that degrades my brain
We call it nothing but age
They call it expiry date

Call me thirty plus
Family, friends and all
Asking what's wrong?
You have it all
Still without man after all

Call me thirty plus
Determines nothing but fate
It chases as life fades
Haunted us for years
Practised by typical male

Call me thirty plus
With all concerns raised
Adorned to chase men with disgrace
In search for surname
Gains shelled body with shattered brain

Call me thirty plus
Without my consent
Tagged as infertile
Tinned with caution
Labelled medically unknown

Call me thirty plus
Bald, old and obese
Apparently Prince Charming of this age
Rejected my hand without gaze
Saying too old for his grace

Call me thirty plus
Charmingly netting a trap
Womaniser as it sounds
Me avoiding the cage without rage
Still called slut even with chaste

Call me thirty plus
Wrinkled youth with truth
Suffocated to death
Without matter of act
Shamed and blamed for every breath

Call me thirty plus
Worked until my last breath
To survive as a fact
A human being not a dirty act
With death sentence at age of wreck

Call me thirty plus
Aged with shame
Harassed by traditional game
Foresee generations without gain
Surviving through pain with thirty plus name

Faiza

Truth

Lies and hate
Running wild
This life has sealed its fate
Time can never wait
Alone and full of despair
This nightmare cannot continue
A shattered life
Hope is gone today
Faith will remind us one day
Because that bell will sound
For we need to pray
Open our eyes
Look at what we have become
Think with your head
Never your heart
Believe there is more to come
Forget light and darkness
See beyond that burning sun

Michael James Hurst

This Place I Call Home

I live in the county of Surrey
A place that's leafy and green
Carshalton is where I call home
And was once even fit for a queen
Anne Boleyn she frequented these quarters
And down the road is Anne Boleyn's well
On riding her horse through the village
Her horse it took to a rear, the beast it came down heavily
Thus causing Anne Boleyn's spring to appear.
We've the lovely Oaks Park on the doorstep
An estate once owned by Derby's 12th Earl
While dining with friends one evening
He decided to give horse racing a whirl
The Earl entered his own horse called Bridget
And to the joy of the Earl his horse won
Well the rest is really history but this is how the famous Epsom Derby begun.
We're famous here for our lavender, once the best in the world
When the fields are in bloom it's amazing, a beautiful sight to behold.
A stroll down Carshalton village and the ponds will not fail to delight
Brimming with wildlife by day, twinkling in the moonlight at night.
And Carshalton House, what a building! I must say I'm not one to boast
But it's an amazing Queen Anne mansion
And the Peatling Papers, say it even has ghosts!
One is a murdered housemaid, and the butler re-enacts his gruesome crime.
The other is a murdered taxman who died from a broken spine
He was thrown downstairs by the owner, who he looks for all of the time
But his search will always be futile, and his bill can never be paid
So he'll walk the house forever, along with the poor murdered maid.
Now that's my small introduction to Carshalton
You're so welcome to come here and roam
See all the places I've not listed, the place I love to call home.

Trudy Simpson

From The Cradle To The Grave

In infancy they hung from mobiles above our cots.
They were our first companions as cuddly toys.
In rhymes, bedtime stories, and early learning books,
puppets, cartoons and sing-a-longs.

From nursery wallpaper – to
our gardens, ponds, farms and parks
where we fed the ducks, swans and geese.

On birthday cakes, paper plates, cups,
spoons, feeding bowls and motifs on clothes.
Fishing trips, nature centres, zoos,
donkey and pony rides – to our first pets.

Penguin, Ladybird, Disney and Beatrix Potter,
The Brothers Grimm, Hans Christian Anderson,
TV, cinema, poetry, pictures, paintings, photo snaps.

Transfers, stickers, pens, pencils, erasers, sharpeners,
straws, toothbrushes, glasses, mugs, lunch boxes.
Paperweights, door stops, cards and games.

Scarves, socks, slippers and onesies.
Tales told around the hearth, campfire or Bonfire Night.
Of werewolves, bloodsucking bats and black demon dogs.

Sculptures, statuettes, ornaments and carvings.
They are found in emblems, logos, shields and badges,
tattoos, jewellery, tapestries, needlework and buttons.
Curtains, cushions, pillows, blankets and rugs.

Animals are all around us, seeping into every part of our lives.
Don't tripwire the end for them –
Treasure them.

Elaine Christie

Let Time Stop

Let time stop
As your tiny luscious eyes
Blink in the first light
And new life begins

Let me hold this moment
Of over-powering love
Life fragile but strong
A celebration of joy
My heart bursts with song

Let time stop
As lips first touch
A fleeting, nervous kiss
Innocence and bliss

Let me hold this joy
Of first love's beating heart
Of hands clasped tight
Into the night
As blushing girl meets boy

Let time stop
In love's embrace
And waking in your arms
Feeling safe from harm

Let passion race
And never stop
As two unite as one
And in our hearts and souls
A single light is shone

Let time stop
As you take your final breath
Ragged, rasping
Gasping for life

Let me hold it
Bitter-sweet
Hold on to this final
Moment of life
Hold on to you

But time stops for no man
Nor child
Nor even death

And as it passes by
Each fleeting moment fades
But does not die

But as for me
I grasp these fleeting
Breaths of time
Like stolen treasures
Locked away in my mind
Brought out, recalled
Savoured, enthralled
In darkness and in quiet

For each memory held dear
Of joy or love or pain

Becomes a seed, a promise
And a sign
That in the wake of passing time
Life and love go ever on
Ever new and ever strong
As forward rolling on and on
Time – don't stop!

David Babatunde Wilson

The Immortal Mind Of The Mountain Farmer

I wither, with her,
In this house of mine,
Where there is something lacking,
In my sun-dried sap of mind.
We both climb behind,
The vineyards of listening leaves,
That whisper themselves,
To all the mighty sugar pine trees.

Here, where the blossom stands,
We hold Nature's holy hands,
Before this house of mine,
That teases me as spring unwinds,
The owed overhaul of the floral fireflies.
As the boring burning,
Of the sun on my windowpanes,
Exempts me from any quarrel,
From competing in a smouldering game,
With my western jazz-ridden name,
As we loiter on a life that is gloriously tame.

Here, where my wife withers,
In this house of mine,
And bathes in her butter oil,
Listens to the violent overbearing twist,
Of her birth-controlled turmoil,
Distracting herself from her withered all,
And on her nose, there she sits,
The witchcraft worthy boil.

We could not tell you,
Oh, but of the world outside,
From this house of mine,
Or whether we are contempt,
With Nature's well wishing attempts . . .

For there are mountains,
Spread avant-garde, along, around,
O! But we both fear to look down,
Over waterholes weary and old,

Perhaps for us the sheep decide to graze,
On early morning altitude days,
And the trees are invading,
With the clouds in the sky protecting.

So, it is faithless, also frightening,
Tinged with sickening, seductive, sublime,
In this cabin, this shed, oh holy dread,
My immortal head, this house of mine.

Louis Glazzard

Otherworld

I reach my hand upward. Riddled with sadness, a crow carries off my soul into
the afterlife
As tears roll vengeful thoughts, burdened with strife
Beside my corpse, Morigan is perched on a branch of a nearby tree
Waiting to feed on my rotting flesh, after the battle ends
My soul prays to Rhiannon to save me, with her birds that sing healing chords
But for me this is not what she intends
Harmoniously her birds bring my decaying bones to their feet
Enchanted, I dance under the moonlight, for it is the last night of November
Now I realise death is something I cannot cheat
But for this night each November, I am told I may return in splendour

Once again, I am carried back to the Underworld now my dance here is over
Full of despair and pain for my evil deeds, for me there is no composure
Irusan's fierce eyes pierce my soul, through his fiery pits of Hell
Shape-shifting alongside us, casting his judgement spell
At the end of my journey stands a mirror and the calming scent the essence of
nightshade
Waiting for me in the mirror is not my reflection
But the Goddess Cheridwen with her cauldron decorated with jade
As she reaches through the portal to take my hand, she says. 'For you there is
no rejection.'
Now my dance with the faeries in the other world has begun
For all my good deeds are praised under the midnight sun

Aiysha Homer

Spare Electricity

The night is at its most electric towards 3am;
brilliant, eager and buzzing
above the playground on the hill.

It is some thousand strides from the house where I lie now;
that playground with the red swing that used to loosen my heartstrings
like shoelaces;
back when biscuit cupboards were mountain tops,
and I was always eating sunshine,
photosynthesising,
charging, and charging fields -
always letting light in.

That electric dark is currently occupied by rabbits,
brilliant, eager and buzzing,
dancing under freckled planets.
The night can't help but smile,
as they may roll the moon to their warren for breakfast,
crack it against the horizon; a yolky sunrise,
an omelette Sunday sky.

All this talk of morning and I'll yawn,
rub my eyes like the conkers I kept,
warm the frail blood in my lids,
the currents,
caught between the sun and seeing.
There was blood between school trousers and grazed knees,
there is blood in those selfsame rabbits too
and my dog smells it, charges forward,
when we walk fourteen hours later.
I might trip. I still do;
now, over people.
Once you're tall your fall is harder,
and lasting Bambi-clumsiness makes coordinating any kind of romance,
a game of trodden toes, two left feet on ice, blindfolded.
But when I see you,
I kaleidoscope.

And then the horizon is a Turner painting,
populated by my ideas lit wild and Emin neon, all the train ride home.
All I see is a split galaxy,
hands through shirt folds, nails against pink and chrome.

You were nebulous once.
I was ambitious. Persistence is admirable in conkers,
less so in lovers.

I admit, we are brilliant,
eager, buzzing still.
My jump lead lips insist,
perhaps driven by possibility,
or rabbits running circuits under our feet -
I am conducting their spare electricity
and experiments in my sleep.
When the night is at its most electric, towards 3am,
I am kept up considering if my heartstrings
are loose enough now, to let a little of that kept light out.
Whether I am charged,
whether I am bright enough,
you just might see a spark in me yet.

Simon Marshall

The Wolf And His Mountain

This tale begins with a mountain,
So high;
Covered in rain,
And frost,
But those who venture,
Are found only to become lost.
Next in this tale,
There lived a man,
Who would follow every trail,
And every narrow bridge,
To find a way to reach the top of the mountain.
However what he did not realise,
Is that for each step he took,
There was a creature who,
Lingered behind him, resembling
The main villain from a child's book.
'Why?' I hear you say,
The creature was nothing more than a wolf,
Who had great big teeth,
Perfect to eat the man with.
Each and every day the wolf would see,
If anyone had belief in the myth,
Of the mountain and the wolf,
Where if one human man reaches the top,
On a full moon,
He will transform into a mystical creature,
Also known as a werewolf.
Many of the intrigued villagers have tried,
Only to become nothing more than a trophy,
To represent the wolf's pride.
The man suddenly heard a shriek,
As the wolf became weak,
'I must be close,' the man laughed,
'What gave you that idea?' the wolf sniggered.
This tale ends with a happy note,
But for who, the wolf or the man?

Amie Jones

Absence In The Throne Room

On that stormy night we left the castle,
Out the back door, we made no hassle,
Fires still burning, beds unmade,
Two boys with lion hearts, we were unafraid,
Our quarters now empty, only memories inside,
Of fruitful existences of glory and pride,
For we were the princes of Blackbird Fall,
Fearsome in battle, the girls would crawl,
But what could be said for grand halls, shiny armour,
Only lies, silver trays and unnecessary drama,
We craved something more than kinghood alone,
To go beyond and afar, see the road less known,
And besides which one of us would be Father's true heir,
One destined to rule, one destined to despair,
Not us, not we, we stand strong as brothers,
Forsaking all jewels, all crowns, all lovers,
Dressed in our underclothes, we fled that night,
Hidden in the gardens until morning light,
The cold rains poured, the angry winds whistled,
Warning the castle of our premature dismissal,
Dawn brought with it the Queen's sweet sobs,
Her two sons had vanished, send out the dogs,
Their search was long and thorough and wide,
'I do not understand,' our poor father sighed,
Our sudden disappearance certainly was a mystery,
The lost Princes of Blackbird, our story made history,
All titles, all burdens, from which we are now freed,
Foreign sands and fresh waters, we hunt deer, we drink mead,
Royal restraints and relations cast onto the tide,
Our wanderlust cured, new lands at our side,
We are gone, we are dead, and we've abandoned our post
And to our splendid absence brother, I'll give a toast,
Unshaven, untidy, we lay under the stars,
And thank the Gods high above us, for bringing us this far,
Dearest Mother and Father sit inside stone,
Two strapping men short of inheritance to the throne,
Questions unanswered, no words left to say,
Our kingdom gone quiet, a million miles away.

Elizabeth Frances Garnett

Memory Of A Grandfather

12-year-old Beatrice had often listened to stories about her grandfather. Her mother told how her grandmother, Beatrice's namesake, received a telegram telling of his death. The fishing boat that rescued him off Dunkirk had been blown up when he thought he was safely on his way home. He was 23 years old.

On the 70th anniversary of VE Day, Beatrice secretly took her grandfather's medals from her parents' room, and pinning them on, left home. She took her best ribbon, along with her pocket money, bought a bunch of roses from the corner shop and tied the ribbon around them. At the War Memorial, she looked at the names, with tears running down her cheeks, reading her grandfather's name.

As she placed the flowers and medals on the steps, an old gentleman in uniform took her gently in his arms, asking where she lived. Taking her hand he took her safely home, after ensuring the medals were in her pocket, leaving her at her door.

Earlier, her frantic mother had phoned her husband and friends. She was about to call the police when Beatrice arrived home. Later that evening, talking with her parents, she was convinced the old gentleman was her grandfather. Then feeling something in her pocket, she found the medals. 'But how could they be here, I left Grandpa's medals at the memorial?'

Later, in bed, she said a prayer for the 'kind gentleman', knowing she had finally met her grandfather.

Janis Gwynn

What Is Love?

Some say it's in the gentle breeze.
In summer skies, streaked with pink.
Some say it glistens in a winter freeze.
I say it's in the way we fall in sync.

I've heard it said, it's in the stillness of the night.
In moon and stars, glittering in the sky.
I've heard it is present at first light.
I say, it's how we hate to say goodbye.

I've read it's in the morning's first sip of tea.
Or in that delicious dish they say is so divine.
I've read it is sunlight, twinkling on the ripples of the sea.
I think it's how I'm yours and you are mine.

Some say it's in the setting sun.
Or in the pleasure of a choice.
Some say it's when you're having fun.
I say, it's in the sound of your voice.

I know it's everywhere and all around us now.
I know I feel it and I'm certain you do too.
Some say love is all the beauty of the world.
I say, together . . . we are love . . . me and you.

Danielle Angela Pegg Mowbray

These Hands

Whose are these younger hands I've come to know?
Loving hands that lift my eiderdown
Over spheres of pain with ancient names,
Liver-spotted shoulders, ripe with age;
Not callous, yet callous all the same.

Recall the time you first beheld your fists,
Clench and then unclench like budding May.
Small, unseen, unworried and pristine,
Strong enough to carry your own pens,
Their ink the only stain you had to clean.

Your fingers smooth and delicate might trace
Whorls and lines and notches of your fate;
Imitate palms of hands on palmy sands,
Writing both your names inside a heart.
Ephemeral joys you mark and understand.

Before my hands knew love they had to work:
Blistered while they bore my humble trade;
Splintered should I go against the grain;
When I met your mother, how they shook!
How honoured our success succeeds our pain.

Oh Heaven, please let them remember how
These two tired hands did set in motion
Lives so far and wide entire tides
Couldn't swipe their sand-scribed names,
Or the father's love I hold for them besides.

Dan Hartigan

The Wheel

It was the eldest's idea.
The shooting range, combining guns and giant teddies
(her twin passions) proved magnetic.
A sticky day, and the kids fizzing over like Coke cans.
Five pounds admission.

Husband does not like the fair.
The cheap tricks, cheap thrills, expensive burgers.
We feed the twins soft blue sugar.
Hard red sugar for the eldest.
Inflatable slides, dodgy-looking carousel, consolation prizes, grumbles, hook-
a-duck, eye-rolls.

Twilight now, and all the colours less obnoxious.
The air cools, causes shivers
like fingernails tracing patterns, idle.
Lights bounce off husband's teeth.

All three kids in the bouncy castle -
Time enough, just, for the Ferris wheel.
That upward swoop.
That waiting, like looking at an almost-full moon.

Nothing is what it used to be, fairs included
but a wheel is a wheel
is a wheel.
And the peak of a wheel
was always our small kingdom.

Lizzy Huitson

Life As A Labyrinth

There are many people in this world,
But this poem is about one person,
A very ordinary person,
In a very unordinary simile.

Life at the starting line seems easy,
Like when you first enter a labyrinth, otherwise known as a maze
You see the straight line ahead of you, and follow it,
But life isn't one straight line, nor is a labyrinth.

As a child, the labyrinth is wonderful,
Full of space and freedom,
The beauty encompasses you,
There's never really any dull moments.

Suddenly, you're a teenager and confronted by your first dead end,
At first glance turmoil and stress becomes you,
You achieved a C when,
You thought it deserved an A.

So, you walk in another direction,
Or otherwise find a new way to achieve an A,
The hedges slowly open up and years pass by,
The line seems quite straight now as qualifications drop by.

Those hedges, you never quite took notice of them,
You look up and they're intimidating, like your boss at work,
But, you soon learn that they guide you from place to place,
So that you are ahead of what people call the 'human race'.

Competition and desire, it keeps you ahead
To find the end, your dreams, a way out of the Labyrinth
And so you run, you run through the maze almost finding your dreams
And you fall, they've rejected you, them all.

The world is full of people,
Those who hate and snigger,
Or those who just about help you,
And you're back on your feet, not running, but walking, fast.

Marriage, children, friends,
You did it because you learn what it means to love,
And soon generations walk through the same labyrinth,
That you have once taken too

You've turned many corners in your life,
So suddenly your way out of your 'troubled life' is just ahead,
The way out of the maze is in front of you,
But you don't take it.

No, reflect on the end that you've always wanted,
So suddenly getting there was the best part
Life is not like a labyrinth
It isn't trapping you and offering only one way out,
But in many ways, there is only one way out

Hope.

Some people make it far in the maze, in life
Some never make it far enough,
But where there's a start, there's an end
The end is not necessarily death.

Survival isn't getting to the end,
It's acknowledging that there is an end,
That end is knowing there's a way out of troubles,
And that way out troubles implies hope.

You survive life as a labyrinth,
Because you always hope that one day you'll make it to your dreams,
Even if you don't, this hope drives you to meet dead ends and new directions,
And soon, you realise that life, whether complicated or thrilling,
It's a labyrinth in blessing.

Nishita Choudhury

A Haiku About Soup

I will drink my food,
when all of my teeth are gone.
Until then . . . I'll chew.

Anna Jacob

Good Fences

New neighbours have moved in to the house at the back of ours. For years the house had been hidden behind a green screen of conifers, with only the red tile rooftop exposed reminding us that it was still there. Within a week of their arrival, the Mackenzies had cut down the trees and hauled them away along with our privacy.

Suddenly it's like we're living in an episode of that old TV programme 'The Land of the Giants'. Well alright, that might be a slight exaggeration. I seem to recall the humans only being about the size of a pepper pot. I may be short but thankfully I'm not that small.

Bizarrely though it's not even as though my neighbours are particularly tall. I met them in the street once, yes I looked up to them but only as much as I look up to anyone. I don't think I'll ever have the opportunity to look down my nose at anyone.

Nevertheless when they step outside into their back garden they seem to grow as they approach the fence. It's like they suddenly turn into nine foot giants, either that or they can levitate.

Of course, Tom has a much more boring rationale for this miraculous event that we witness each day. He's never been very imaginative. He simply calls it decking.

Amanda Warner

The Hunter

His ears rang with Afghanistan. He knew the sounds of AK-47s and Stingers ripping against bone and metal would never leave him. Even less so the cries of his comrades as they breathed their last, limbs separated from bodies, insides spilling onto the dry earth. The worst sounds of all were the cries of those mutilated by the Mujahideen as warnings; arms cut off at the shoulders, men forced to crawl back to base with their feet having been hacked off at the ankles. But it was the sound of matrimonial bliss that was now keeping him awake. The sound of two bodies moving on very rusty bedsprings. It was preferable to the alternative, the sound of matrimonial arguments, usually drunken. That had come earlier. But one came after the other as surely as night followed day. Now, his newlywed neighbours were very much back in love with each other.

He padded to the kitchen and poured himself a vodka in the hope it might help him sleep.

It didn't. He coughed. A jagged line of pain ran from his neck, through his left earlobe and multiplied at the base of his cranium. He shook his head, as though to disperse the tingling sensation. He reached for his gun. It was time to do what he did best.

He closed the door to his flat and climbed down the stairs. He let himself out into the warm spring evening and headed for the forest. Killing usually made him feel better.

Adam Cook

Forget Me Not

This is a cruel and tormented kind of love,
A love with no bounds,
Yet such love as this, is enchanting,
And I fall without realizing,
I'm dwelled into madness,
As I sacrifice my sanity,
I give everything to you,
A power only you hold,
A love I call a curse,
Yet I don't want this to end,
I never asked for such love,
Yet I'm in debt with fate,
I'm his very own muse,
I am only for him,
As he is only for me,
He is mine.
A heaven's creation I can call my own,

Your skin,
Your touch,
Why am I so addicted?
Your fingertips cold to my hot-blooded body,
You make my hairs stand on end,
I'm shocked in place,
Waiting – Just waiting for you to have me,
As you cool me down, I warm you up, the perfect fit,
A drug to me,
And I get more and more greedy to have you,
Enough will never be enough,
Time stops and this moment is held in place,
Then realisation crawls in slowly,
Like death taking its victim,
Each second that passes is a lifetime,
My heart panics,
My hands are moist,
My breath shortens,
Then these voices overpower my thoughts,
My body sinks,
My throat tightens,
Whispers on top of whispers,

'You have to leave me,'
'I can't have you,'
I can only call you . . . mine for
One, last, night . . .

I can see it in your eyes,
You don't want to leave,
But this fate likes to play with us,
The last chapter, our final memory,
I can hear the fireworks,
As we move as one,
Your voice, is music to my ears,

I see you,
Only you,
As this world crumbles around us
Brick by brick,
Kiss by kiss,
Your taste is sweet enough,
A linger of hope,
Desperation, I have no control,
As I'm slowly losing you,
An endless hunger that I cannot satisfy,
As this night is not everlasting,
I capture you, one last time,
Lastly you smooth your fingers over my face and then through my hair,
Excitement alights me once more,
A spark that can never again be lit by you,
Your longing stare into my eyes,
We know time is soon upon us,
I close my eyes to try not let any tears escape but I failed
Everything go into darkness . . .

Time has caught up with me,
I see stars disappear one by one,
My eyes open and disappointment is the first I feel,
The dawn is upon me and I am rushed with loneliness,
Tears fall, my cheeks are flushed,
The scent of him is still around me and I close my eyes to see him once again,
I smile for you; I'm at ease of this suffering,
His kiss, imprinted in time
Last night -
Is like a dream of a dream that I will always remember,

My love,
My life,
My everything,
Forget me not . . .

R.J Whitley

Is It A Sin?

Is it a sin to go out and get drunk,
Run away from home and do a bunk?
Is it a sin to go to war and kill,
Shoot someone dead just for the thrill?
Is it a sin to puncture your skin,
To reach that high you seek from within?
Is it a sin when you break someone's heart,
Even if you didn't really want to part?
Is it a sin to have a child so young?
Don't worry you'll not be the only one.
Is it a sin to stand up to a bully?
Let everyone know it'll stop the worry.
Is it a sin to cheat or to steal?
Maybe it was part of the deal.
Life must go on sinful or not,
It's up to us all to help stop the rot.
As generations move on year after year
Put your foot down now make it easier to bear.
So lay down the bombs, guns and knives
Get some humanity and freedom back in our lives.

Dawn Williams-Sanderson

Like Silence Through A Fish-Eye Lens

Through roots and leaves the leaving routes the day behind you now
Sinking fast the light recedes through neon night to stellar plough
Where cryptic clues in package stash behind the doors of dreams
Lead you through the maze of days between daylight's woven beams
That breathe the sun's beguiling light in pulsating chlorophyll
The toothless tiger whose keeper caged refuses to keep still
Will drain the hearts and sap the wood behind the schoolyard wall
And exhale the night into the world where trip will turn to fall
The calculated paths of falling birds will root themselves in lore
And chequered patterns proliferate on littered forest floor
Where cats with cataracts hold court for acolytes of Freud
And long dead faces rise once more to fill the memory void
Raising dust the red rust horns of stampede metaphor
They pierce the posing purple sides of pampered matadors
Whose gleaming swords can't pierce the myths we all believe are true
And ring the planet's Saturn soul to steal a moon or two
The mathematical significance of hungry babies' cries
Will solve the riddles propagated by childhood's long demise
And cards that lie face down with all their colours calling
Won't stop the crumbling walls of sleep from accidentally falling
Into the arms of long-lost friends and parliaments of rust
Whose scattered voices choke back tears that trail a line of dust
Through all that you know and all you need and all that you want to be
And wash you clean to leave you free the rising day to see
Now you return with the sunrise mind all cottoned by the ride
Fingers grasp the garbled messages cast up by the tide
But words on dreamscape paper writ will crumble in the light
And falling through the clouds will echo things you can't put right

Garth Erickson

Untitled

We all have our secrets,
we all have our reasons,
we all have our angels
we all have our demons,
we all have a way,
though sometimes we get lost,
remember to cherish what we have,
and love 'it', 'them', or 'that' the most.
One day you could wake up and find your dreams have passed you by,
Then the rest of your life ends up being a lie.
Hold on to the memories but forgive your mistakes,
learn from them, then move on,
one step is all it takes.
Move forward with hope,
leave your heartache behind,
open your heart,
who knows what you'll find.

Emma Thompson

Stormy Weather

The boat was sinking, just round the headland from the harbour; the catch
was lost. Ed and David, the two man crew, struggled together through the
tempestuous sea to the shore where they sheltered in a cave they knew of old.
Dawn came with the promise of a warm, sunny day. Ed and David clambered
wearily up the cliff path. Their boat's mast and soggy pennant were still visible
and had been seen. Exhausted, they reached the top of the cliff. There was a
car approaching over the short cliff-top grass. It stopped and Ed's wife Mary
jumped out, ran to him and flung her arms round him, laughing and crying
with relief and joy. There was no sign of David's wife, Connie.
'Where's Connie?' he asked anxiously, his eyes scanning the landscape
around.
Mary immediately turned to him with a beaming smile. 'In hospital,' she
replied jubilantly, 'the maternity wing! Congratulations Dave, you have a son, a
beautiful seven pound son.'

Jacqueline N Fogwill

What I Love About Britain

I love the fact you can be anonymous
And people leave you alone
I love the fact that you can go anywhere
And Britain is a place you can call home

It's easy to get around
Whether you walk, ride or have a car
You can easily go anywhere
There is no place too distant or far

We have a welfare state
That supports people in need
We have a great place called London
Full of multi-culture and diversity

We have many tourists
That come to this beautiful country
Compared to some parts of the world
We are darn right lucky

The winters may be rough
And summers can be overwhelming
But as long as I have a place I can call home
That's enough to keep me smiling

Franklin Brady

Lost The Plot

Untidy, too large, overgrown,
Abundance of unwanted invasions.
Down-trodden and shabby, ill-kempt;
An assault on discerning sensations.

Crave roses to blush summer's face,
Long-legged sunflowers teasing the sky,
The caress of blue iris eyes,
But, lo, low, lowly with weeds, there I lie.

Betty Williams

'And We Have Known Them . . .'

And we have known them ever,
for of our best we gave,
the prides of fighting fathers,
the glorious and the brave;
As boys we gave them men's hard suits,
put in their hands our guns,
and to the trenches gave we up,
our brothers and our sons;
Just boys dressed all as soldiers,
as if they were at play,
on trains from North Road station,
we saw them all away;
Their mothers' faces wet with tears,
their hearts filled all with dread,
as if reflect the windows there,
the faces of the dead.

In Devonport we cheered them,
upon the gangplanks bare,
as 'pon those grey behemoths,
they thronged and postured there;
We dressed them in our sailor suits,
and piped them off to war,
to bleed and breathe and choke their last
abaft some foreign shore;
Asteer their mighty dragons,
of iron, brass and steel,
to roar and crash and thunder,
beneath the reaper's heel;
All sleeping 'neath the boiling sea,
and deaf now to the cost,
of Weston Mill and Efford Field
soiled high with Plymouth's lost.

We cheered and waved them over,
those string and canvas birds,
awing across the Channel,
all deaf our earthbound words;
With fathers' hearts swelled all with pride,

and words caught hard their throats,
'til far horizons swallowed them,
and stilled their engines' notes;
'Til hawks we slipped their jesses,
and threw them to the skies,
to hunt the clouds o'er Flanders,
to be the gunners' eyes;
But never more the gauntlet,
the best of them would know,
save one cold line a bronz'ed plaque,
stood proud on Plymouth Hoe.

We did not know their terrors,
their bleak skies rained with fear,
no shell nor bomb nor bullet,
fell hot and rested here;
But laid they waste the three old towns,
to scythe with death their kin,
'til not one family stood complete
that lived those bounds within;
No night a church bell silent,
nor pyre to quench its flames,
and not one morn forgiven,
its taken and their names;
No churchyard for one night undug,
nor chapel step untrod,
or day no Plymouth's home brought child,
was laid beneath its sod.

But rest they now as shadows,
in mem'ries and in prayers,
they shall not know their children,
nor shall they know their heirs;
Though monuments to Heaven raise,
they will not see them now,
nor will they glimpse on Armistice day
our grateful heads abow;
Those Plymouth sons and daughters,
who shall not come again,
inscribed upon our foreshores,

for all time shall remain;
And we have known them ever,
for of our best we gave,
the prides of fighting fathers,
the glorious and the brave . . .

Sullivan The Poet

Underneath

Beneath the surface
Hidden deep within
Lie my biggest triumphs
Lie my greatest sins

Beneath the surface
Where I hide so well
The place my thoughts jump lively
The place my feelings dwell

Beneath the surface
A different me you'll find
One without a filter
Or rules to hide behind

Beneath the surface
If you dare to look that far
I'm completely open
I bare my every scar.

Nikki Elskamp

Her Maiden Voyage

With a length of 882 feet and weight of 45000 ton
Her great skyline height would shadow the beaming sun.
She set for her maiden voyage, April 10th 1912,
From Southampton to New York she would set sail.
Passengers from first class to third would gather through
the metal doors expecting a new life soon.
She carried 2,223 people on her luxury decks
but the lack of lifeboats was a link to a series of events.
Money got short so steel rivets were replaced
Iron ones were used therefore adding to the mistakes.
Storage space was low, objects were packed in
making the chances of finding things very slim,
Binoculars were lost so icebergs were hard to find
this is another key event that sank this White Star Line.
The Captain thought of a quicker route to shorten her maiden trip
But after making this decision the iceberg would shortly hit.
Six iceberg warnings were sent hours before
but then one eventually hit at 11:44
People ran riot to get the women and children on the boats
the other 2/3 of the passengers could only wait and hope
She eventually went down after 160 minutes of terror
Taking men, women, children and families down with her
The unsinkable ship went down in vain
also with screams, tears, horror and pain
The ship that was supposed to make dreams and new lives
took them instead but people's love for her never dies.
So the ship that weighed 45000 tons with 90ft beams
was called Titanic or The Ship of Dreams.

Meghan Cooley

The Little Boats

Men waited in the cold sea.
Water up to their necks you see.
A fighter plane fired at them.
No shelter could they find, those men.

Men on the shore tried to help.
Shooting as the planes flew by.
Not wishing their comrades to die.

On the high seas, destroyers then.
Sent out their boats for those men.
Brave British and French allies.
Waiting there I tell no lies.

Then much to their dismay.
Those large ships sailed away.
Quietness then descended there.
Brave men in the sea despaired.

Suddenly there was a cry.
Lookouts there did e-spy.
The little boats have come by.
From England now I do not lie.

Many men were saved that way.
On our little boats they were I say.
Many taken from the sea.
Soaking wet, cold, but free.

Free from all that turmoil so.
Now afloat and homeward bound.
The British Army safe and sound.
Not all of course, as some did stay.
Fighting, to hold, Germans at bay.
So their friends could get away.

Leave this blessed killing ground.
Return to England safe and sound.
As them little boats did us grand.

Now years later boats do go.
To those beaches now aglow.
With those spirits that we know.
Of brave British men and so,

172

Sound your horns, ring the bells,
For you in little boats did so well.
Captains of little boats too,
Deserve the praise of each of you.

Thank you all for answering the call.
To save our army was that call.
The army was of our men.
Brave souls were all of them.

Those that survive now are old.
But memories they have now told.
Of those little boats on the sea.
Who, thank God, saved our army

Where, you ask did they lurk?
Off the beaches, of Dunkirk.

As I sit in the comforts of my house, I feel humbled by the actions of all those men in their little boats. How brave it was of them ordinary civilians with probably no military training to go into such a den of iniquity. I daresay we'll never be able to offer sufficient thanks. Let us hope we are never called to do such a thing again.

The Mad Author (Stanley R Harris)

Gallipoli

There was no dust, no sand, no dirt, no stench, no dead bodies for me to clear.
At Sulva Bay
Just fear.
That's what we shared.
And knowing that the world is no longer safe.
I too, understand my dear Albert the trauma that you went through
The shock, the numbness, the deadness in your soul.
The hypervigilence, a sense of danger that follows you wherever you go.
The unbearable stress and tension – you cannot ever relax
For fear of another attack.

And when you returned, nothing had changed.
You felt just the same wherever you were, still traumatised.
And even after this, when you were sent back, you were fighting another war.
An inner war.
An inner war, inside you, eating and rotting your body and soul.
You were down-trodden but you did not know why this was so.
There were no words to describe how you really felt.
And there was no one to whom you could tell
Because you had to be brave as soldiers are, until that moment when you fell
On the 1st September, 1918 at the Battle of the Somme
Far from Gallipoli where your trauma begun.

You were blown up sky-high only to be found lying face down
In a field nearby among the many thousands of men
Frozen in the still of night
A duty done
Another life gone.

Patricia Aubrey

The Silent Observer

Our eyes meet, for a split-second you made me jump. Pulse quickening, a heat rush surged through my body... or was it a hot flush...? We stared at each other. Eyes never leaving one another. Every move I made you calculated it, followed it analysed it! Never letting me out of your sights!

I feel the hot flush again... yet when I looked directly at you, you acted as if you hadn't seen me.

I pace the floor not quite sure how to deal with you. Breath quickening, I pluck up the courage to get closer to you. I feel the adrenaline rush or is it that hot flush...? But I can't approach you...

I take my glass in hand, steady myself, hands fumbling, I have to be brave! This moment won't last forever! I approach you but for a moment you have disappeared from view. I retreat back to my seat crestfallen!

Maybe I should just welcome you, accept you, the silent observer. But I've met your type before, a predator, with those long legs, that dark hair, deep penetrating eyes that dig deep into my soul. You entice your prey into the invisible web woven around you. Captured, enslaved, entangled in your grasp...

But how am I going to deal with you? You return to your place where you can observe the room, not missing a movement or me! The adrenaline rush, or another damn hot flush surges through me again! I'll make another drink! I know if I leave the room you will be gone by the time I return. How will I know where to find you? It's not as if I can call you up!

I need a pee! Desperately! I cross my legs, still with our eyes never leaving each other. Neither of us making the first move!

With quivering hand and empty glass I approach you, another heat rush surging through my body... chest heaving, adrenaline coursing through my veins. Our eyes never leaving each other...

Now it is you who is to be encapsulated, trapped, your fate now in my hands! Oh spider how brave I am!

Trudi Mackie-Brown

The Landlord's Lament

A slightly eccentric gentleman,
attired in an electric blue suit,
wanders across the fields
doffing his hat to the people he meets.

The bright yellow rape seed
and overcast sky
make the gentleman wish he'd been born
with the lyrical dexterity of Jay-Z or Keats.

And as he follows the footpaths
like a seasoned rambler,
dodging deposits from four-legged friends
he comes across a pub he once did frequent.

Out of place amongst the blue collar workers
he orders a pint of dubious taste,
settles on a bar stool
and finds himself listening to the landlord's lament.

'We had some good times here at 'The Plough'
but the market changed . . . look at it now.
The pints that were pulled, the revelry known,
now the seeds of its demise have sadly been sown.
The locals rallied with little effect
as all the profits poured down their necks
and so hangs the sale sign . . . it will be no more
so let's have a toast to the barflies of yore.'

The gentleman sunk the amber remains
and bid the man good day
to wander the village
where a traditional inn was tarred with shame.

Across the road, just yards of ale away
stood the old pub's nemesis.
The gentleman entered, ordered pork belly
and drank a lager with a long foreign name.

Gavin Simpson

Different Day

Same shit, different day,
He says to me, pedalling the motorway,
Life doesn't work out like you plan,
Like the love between a woman and a man.
We take the stress, the arguments, the work,
We're trying so hard to climb out of the dirt,
To find better, his coffee shop, my writing,
A room with a view, with better lighting
Than the bulbs to keep the plates hot,
Which we run out because the kitchen forgot.
The finishing at 11:45, restaurant a mess,
And driving home together, to collapse and undress.
These are the only times we have, together and lost,
But the 32 hour dates outweigh the costs.
One day we'll crawl out of the mud, baby,
We'll be free, unstuck, you and me,
Because this first date, first love, stuff is beyond,
But when we win, it'll strengthen our bond.
The parents will stare and sneer in shock,
The teachers will stand, co-workers will mock
Our silly dreams for coming true, and being real,
But we'll be laughing at those still in a deal,
A deal with the Devil, we'll survive soon,
Pick ourselves out of Hell, the sun and the moon,
Us, with our love, and our sex, and our lust,
We'll melt the tills and turn the aprons to dust.
To find happiness even richer than ours,
Would be like finding Heaven, but with a playlist and bar,
Same shit, different day; Not forever, my love,
We are flightless parrots, but soon will be doves.

Evie Taylor

The Doublesman

The traffic lights turn red.
Between the hissing of tyres on melted tarmac he weaves and shouts, 'Hot doubles,' peppered with, 'a dash' or 'plenty'. A call that draws the portraits in rear view mirrors, the casual, the suited, the string vested, the bare chested call to the welcomed crier in red, white and black. The food seller, the freight bike rider playing cat and mouse, he skids on the fossilised rubber, the vending tout, long dubbed – the Doublesman.
In pole position in that static moment of the daily race home, he flashes his golden crowns, pedalling from the laden cart, packaged and penned like a red-topped newspaper, barely hinting at what's inside, until he reaches in, pulls out the skins, slaps on the filling, laces the pepper, and caps it all in. The golden fritters tanned with turmeric and spice sandwich the sprouting channa, merging and mixing the whole, the crumbled, and the pureed. Swept up by the steaming juice they tumble and fall, caught in the wrap of the papered wall. Dressings and seasonings mingle, garlic and geera tingle, a fusion, a relish, topped with scotch bonnet, the essence and aroma of pimento, shado beni, and mango chutney.
A moment to savour, at the present and in our history, a tradition made modern by the place, an episode governed by the lights.
Amber, green, the punters now veiled in fumes toot and hoot to go, the moment passed, the Doublesman berated, the red again awaited.

Stella Meadows

Bereft

'In our age there is no such thing as 'keeping out of politics'. All issues are political issues, and politics itself is a mass of lies, evasions, folly, hatred and schizophrenia.' – George Orwell

I hold a loss in both hands
Shuffle thoughts and search for colour
Cling to values
And skin clawing expressions

Cold, blue bodies fill the room
Processions prepare
To share in hope
At the failing house

Hollow opinions swell
Footsteps hit moving caskets
Tripping on crossed cracks
Doorsteps break hearts

Apathy swings opinion
Away from red shame-vaults
Intentional power takes action
To deliver mournful results

Stephen Daniels

The Olive Branch

A haze around the street lights; summer making its ghostly exit, tiptoeing away backstage. Turning the corner towards the canal, he gazed for a moment at his reflection in the copper-coloured water. His heart felt like it had had all the love wrenched out of it, leaving behind a crater, roots exposed and vulnerable. He tried to remember the good stuff, dressed it in the finest linen and richly embroidered silk. The moon grinned ironically through the trees on the far bank. The first drops of rain began to fall.

The bracken crunched in protest as he walked through a small copse. Gossamer threads quivered delicately in the air and orange leaves hung in clusters, waiting to fall. Opening the door, he walked in and turned on the tap. The water spat into the glass. A lamp projected a jerky yellow light. Switching on the radio, he sat and listened to some music. The words of a song infiltrated his thoughts:

'I'm tossed upon the sea of life
And all the charts are lost
And when the dove returns to me,
I'll get the same report.'

Beads of rain sluiced down the window. A pang of despondency overcame him as he reflected on his self-imposed exile.

'With listing ship I search for land;
The sails look sad and torn.
The compass cannot offer me
Safe passage through the storm.'

He did not hear the dull thud outside. Feathers strewn on the tarmac. Rain water glistening on glass shards.

David Winship

At The Intersection

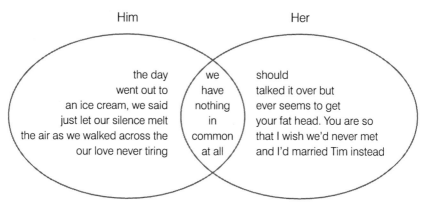

Him   Her

the day   we   should
went out to   have   talked it over but
an ice cream, we said   nothing   ever seems to get
just let our silence melt   in   your fat head. You are so
the air as we walked across the   common   that I wish we'd never met
our love never tiring   at all   and I'd married Tim instead

Brian Bilston

Death

Death. It's inevitable, just like birth.
It's just a question of how, when and how.
I await mine at the right time.
I look back on all the successes and failures, the tears and triumphs and the
loves and losses.
I look at the sky and I think about how I wanted to go, the sunset fading in the
distance along with my life.
I look at my foe. Were his thoughts the same as mine?
I see her coming to collect me. She takes her time. But she comes for all of us
eventually.
I smile, having achieved all I wanted to achieve in this life.
All regrets pass over me like the sea.
Silence now.
She smiles.
She takes the form of my first love.
I smile back.
As my life fades, I feel safe in the knowledge that I lived the life I wanted.
And then it ends.

Charlie Barnes

Prayer For The Resting Souls

The view near the stone is peaceful
and covered with age old memories

Two elderly women sit chatting amidst lost loved ones
content to while away the time in the comfort of precious conversations

The specks of bluebells, dancing daffodils and the meadow of ancient
hardwood trees
give strength and some privacy to this sacred ground

Some stones bowing
Some stones erect
Some stones hiding in shadows
Others broken and abandoned
Some huddled together for support in their grieving

Some still clearly etched with memorials
. . . 'also his wife Sarah Jane died May 20 aged 79 years'

Sunshine and time will wash across these tombstones
Black crow will scavenge between the plots
Nightfall brings eternal rest to those down deep below.

Geraldine Marcellino

Treasured Friends

I'm off to distant shores, my friends -
if only you could see,
a world so calm and beautiful
that's waiting just for me.
But fear not that I go alone,
for deep within my heart,
I'm taking life's sweet memories
in which you played a part.
For everything I meant to you
you meant to me and more,
the joys we shared, time can't erase -
of that you can be sure.
And now my journey's over,
may my love forever stay
in the hearts of all my family
and treasured friends who've walked my way.
So fill your days with laughter,
wear a smile and have some fun!
That's how I hope you'll think of me
in all the days to come.

Valerie Overton-Davies

Electric Blue

As sepia cascaded down,
a spirit flew, and flew,
a potion, a lotion drew,
drew, a tense love apart.

Seasoned by lemony sap,
upsurged with lavender balm,
magnetic it fused the dark,
dark, flowing mesmeric force.

Thumping, black swelling heart,
maroon skies, skin torn apart,
forbidden, just hidden form,
form burning with passion!

Blue room, electric power,
brought you to me, too soon
a flower lay blood red raw,
raw, hair colour of straw.

Weekend tryst, a Cawdor
encounter, embedding our love,
velvet raven wings flew,
flew, shadowing the flame.

Aquamarine merged gold leaf,
a crescendo of silver spray
conquered the canvas, there,
there, a picture of you.

Burnt wood embers died,
our bodies entwined, midst
forbidden fruit, curse forwarded,
forwarded, unwittingly by Eve?

Seasons of dappled shades,
sideways rain, brilliant white snow,
a present for you, brought tears,
tears, a bitter sweet end?

A union as intoxicating as
sweet wine, masqueraded
pretences, scented letters, lay,
lay, unopened, in dusty places.

Old prejudices still remained,
a single rose lay colourless
above a watery grave, goodbye,
goodbye, my electric blue . . .

Christine Evelyn Hawksworth

The London Underground

With frantic speed the human race,
Push and shove to get a space.
Through the open doors they rush
Staggering in the heavy crush.
From the darkened platform roars
A hollow voice of, 'Mind the doors!'
A sudden jolt and we're packed in tight,
Breathing in with all our might.
We thunder through the blackened tube,
In air and heat so thick and crude.
'We're here!' I gasp with great relief,
A station full of more good grief!
'There's no more room,' a man implies,
'You're on my toes,' another cries.
I'm almost forced on someone's lap,
A mystery voice yells, 'Mind the gap!'
There really must be another way,
To reach my office every day.
As long as I am still alive,
Maybe tomorrow I'm gonna drive.

Patricia Guest

My Wish

My wish for you when you're big and tall
is that your dreams are big and your worries small.
Chase your ambitions whatever they may be
Look over your shoulder back to me.
Your loyal champion I'll stand behind
Watching so proudly on a boy who's too kind.

As long as you're happy I'll be so too
In a world full of strangers please just be you.
You're perfect as you are, don't need to rebuild
a character so wonderful, my heart you have filled.
Be confident, be brave, acknowledge mistakes
there'll be triumph and tears and endless heartbreaks.

There'll be decisions, challenges, obstacles too
to overcome in the future to make a better you.
Be tolerant, be kind, if it's all you can be
Be stubborn, be wise, be better than me.
I truly believe in the man you'll become
but you'll always be a baby in the eyes of your mum.

Tracey Robertson

Raised By The Internet

The people on Facebook,
They seem to do it better,
The f**k-me eyes, the camera shots beside the pool (always a cocktail,
an angled umbrella), to beers with the lads (strike a pose, keep it cheeky) and
Everyone is laughing in flashing neon colours,
Playing off seemingly-relaxed observations of others.

Observe their lives – a panoramic movie moment of
Disengagement . . . and then panic because
Am I like them? Do I fit in? Do they like me, do I have as much fun, how do
they look so perfect, how can I be that happy . . .
Is there something wrong with me?

Log off. Rewind. Remind myself -
Internet trends do not correspond to real friends.

Isabelle Kenyon

Style Is Nothing Without The Onlooker

In an evening glove
dazzled to mourning
always pretending as
the afterburn swallows bicycles
ears perked, woodlice on floorboards
creak, my mess streaks
excitement shut out
placing chaos on shelves
organised drama
maze prints surround
searching, bones spun
to make milk, to make
me, make doves
make peace
never recover

under this temporary
blanket.

David Chrzanowski

Truncated Prose

Truncated prose with purpose fluttering
Stops by a jam jar open-toed
''Tis yours fair buttercup,' came the muttering
From the long grass by the road

The summer fly had grazed one ear
Its sound was so discreet
''Tis yours fair buttercup,' to his rear
Did once again repeat

Truncated prose with purpose stuttering
Was now in some distress
''Tis yours fair buttercup,' was spluttering
What got you in this mess?

Anthony R Stevenson

Happiness

I find that happiness is being comfortable
Comfortable with everything that is around you
Being comfortable with family
Just being with them makes me calm
Being comfortable with friends
Smiling, having fun, being equal
Being comfortable with myself
Getting too into a good book
But happiness doesn't mean that everything is perfect
It means that you've decided to look past the imperfections
For happiness is something that comes into our lives
Through doors we don't remember leaving open
You can choose to be happy
When you learn to forget the bad things
Forgive the past and notice the now
Smile, happiness looks good on everyone

Heather Jane Edwards

Homewards

Twisted church spire watches
over brown ridged field
where snow, soft as fur,
nestles in furrows like leverets.
Ink black trees light up from behind
with gold/orange sunset.
Cold kisses my face
leaving rosy imprints.
The road, white with salty sheen,
sings under racing car,
speeding homewards
as day sinks under banks
of snow-swollen clouds.

Vivien Steels

Listening

(I was in hospital with a back injury and I could hear all the visitors arriving . . . and the conversations . . .)

The drift of chatter
searching for ears,
the merry tuned patter
of human sound.

Buzzing and humming
multi-toned vocals
lilt to the ceiling
and stumble to the ground;

solemn, vibrating,
swift never pausing
resonant with tempo
. . . sweet silence now drowned.

Gabriela Alexander

Summer Heat

The dull, flat stillness of the pool
Beneath the somnolent sky,
The steaming heat.
Veiled in the muggy haze
Of the heavy airless midday.

Heavy limbed, tired eyed.
Lank, sticky, clinging
Fibered covered bodies,
Heaving laboriously
Under the oppressiveness.
Gaping, gasping, sprawling
Like dying fish waiting breathlessly,

For a whispered breeze
To waft through
The cloying mugginess,
To relieve the tedium
Of this high summer
Storm-pregnant day.

Anne Bailey

189

Phoenix

My love is complete
Since with you I met
Your tiny hands and feet
My love and heart beat

This is more than fate
It was destiny, my heart
You are a work of art
My shining star, my starlight

To love, with all my might
Kisses, caresses, drops of water sweet
Like summer heat, my heart melts
What is this love, have never felt

My dreams and plans and everything wrought
This love never I thought
Like an oasis in the desert
Magical, like sunlight and sunset

Our lives with you are blest
My every day, my delight
The light under the moonlight
I am lost without

Anna Kapungu

My Secret Wish

If could wish for anything apart from peace on Earth
It would be for the girl with lonely eyes to understand her worth
It would be for all that is bad to just turn into rainbow butterflies
That would wipe away the tears she cries
To help the man with greasy hair reaching for his pipe
Realise he's not old and rotten and that his soul could still be ripe
If only he could fight his demons, troubles and toil
Walk away from those squats and shiny foil
What about that lady sitting on the edge tears pouring
Who has finally cracked all her pain she has been ignoring?
Well I could hold out my hand
Help her to find her grief, help her try to understand
That bad things can happen to good people
And that unfortunately we were not all born equal
So the old lady who is cold and desperate for some heat
Having to choose between warmth or something to eat
My wish would be to help them all
Not a big gesture, something tiny and small
Something that may to others seem irrelevant
But to that person in a hole can be seen as evidence
That things can change, a smile in a crowd can save a person's life
I'd love to pull them out of the darkness and back into the light.

Beth Abbott

Tube Strike

She left the office building
Towards late afternoon,
To get back home to Twickenham,
Despite tube strikes and general gloom.
The day was warm and pleasant,
So she sauntered round the square,
Then turned into Tottenham Court Road,
To catch a bus from there.

A bus rounded the corner -
Quite unexpectedly.
She ran, waving her briefcase,
For the bus driver to see, but
He drove away, ignoring her -
She didn't stand a chance
Against his proud indifference
And supercilious glance.

She ambled down to Oxford Street
And, meanwhile, window-shopped.
There were colourful accessories
- she simply had to stop!
She bought a fine new handbag
In a vibrant shade of rose
And a gorgeous pair of shoes to match,
That didn't pinch her toes.

On reaching Marble Arch
With her new purchases, and case,
She was sweltering, with strands of hair
Adhering to her face.
So she paused to buy a latte
In a bendy cardboard cup,
Then took the cup away with her,
Plus spoon and plastic top.

The traffic in Park Lane was simply
Not moving at all,
But, strolling through Hyde Park,
She found some pleasant shade and cool,
The grass was bliss beneath her feet,
Soft breezes blew her hair

She could walk to Hyde Park Corner,
And might catch a bus from there.

At Hyde Park Corner, traffic stretched
as far as she could see,
But walking was quite fun, instead -
Good exercise, and free,
So she popped along to Harrods -
Just to have a look
And bought a lovely perfume spray
And a glossy cookery book.

She paid for a new holdall
In a green and gold design
To carry all her purchases
And save her space, and time.
She succumbed to some fresh oysters
In the sumptuous Food Hall,
Champagne and chocolate truffles
That weren't too dear at all.

The tube station was firmly closed,
With padlocked folding gates
And bus queues were enormous
- it just wasn't worth the wait,
So, she called in for a lager
At a nearby hostelry -
Relieved that she was single,
Footloose and fancy free.

Her bags were getting heavier,
So she walked more slowly now.
Every single cab was taken
But she'd reach home, anyhow.
At Kensington, she jumped aboard
the first bus she could see,
But it only went to Mortlake -
Just outside the old Brewery.

'I'm not too far from Twickenham,'
She thought. '*It will be fine.*
I should be home for supper,
By half-past eight or nine.'
The bus had dropped her

in a kind of urban No-Man's-Land.
The brewery was there,
But no transport was at hand.

She went up to the flyover
And hailed a taxi cab, then
Piled in with her purchases
All on her seat and lap.
He dropped her off at Twickenham,
Not too far from her flat,
She had to pay a hefty fare,
But didn't grudge him that.

Darkness was falling fast,
As she finally reached home,
Where she guzzled down some water
And put the kettle on.
Her feet were somewhat roughened
From her unaccustomed hike,
But a quick foot spa ensured that they
were soft and velvet-like.

The next day dawned too soon
And brought an added railway strike.
Perhaps she should consider
a small scooter, or a bike . . .
She must commute from Twickenham
Without the tube or train,
But she had done it all before
And she could do it all again!

Sylvia Browning

Empty Playgrounds

Not a creak of a chain
Nor a shout of sheer joy
No swing reaching up to the clouds
Not an intake of breath
From the unpolished slide
Meeting air whooshing up from the ground
Not a thud from the net
Not a ball to be seen
No home goals from lack of direction
No leap into space
From the stout roundabout
No practise for future selection
No jog of the horse
No putt from the course
For the grass is now long and untrodden
No swishing of ropes
No conquering hopes
Needs of childhood . . . have they been forgotten?
Adventure and play
Are the Business of Youth
But where have the children all gone?
To literacy hour or numeracy hour
Or to sit at computers alone.

Mary Froggett

A Farewell Wave

The thin constant line of horizon
And changeable swell of waves
A perpetual flap of white mainsail,
This, all my life, I have craved:

From the creak of dinghy rigging
To the lap against narrow boat hull,
My senses have been with four winds
Or running on tide's ebb and flow.

It's riding on waves of ocean
As salt scented air fills my lungs,
And fighting with roaring storm forces,
Or randomly floating . . . be-calmed,
I've sailed and so often been happy,
Many boats I've known and loved well,
for my spirit is drawn to the seashore
And the sound of a warning buoy's bell.

When summer sun is scorching
Or autumn currents run full,
The call of the sea is unceasing
Her bidding, my heart's constant pull.

So to her I return at life's twilight
Now the burden of living is gone,
To sail the rolling ocean,
At peace . . . for with her I belong.

Bridie Bonello

Ripples

The splash of the water
From parallel lanes
A bald-headed man
With neglected beard
And bloodshot eyes
Struggles to keep
His tongue in his mouth
As the water creates waves
And keeps his body afloat.

His expression is bland
Without grimace or smile
The businessman's thoughts
Are of water and wine
The unmade phone calls
After dinner speech
The signing of contracts
A process complete
The journey home
And the turbulent flight.

Dive bombing children
Disturb the peace
An exit required
A decision to make
Leaving behind
Ripples that meet
Somewhere, some time
To become complete.

Paul A Reeves

The Softest Binding

The envisaged look of disappointment and sorrow on your radiant face,
Is the only thing that stops me from succumbing to the blade's embrace.
The anticipation of anticipation of making you laugh or smile,
Gives me hope that I will feel like a good partner once in a while.
Your insistence on making me alpha of our furry motley pack,
Helps me rail against the burdens that strain my straining back.
Simply put I am nothing,
Yet with you I am entwined with a glorious cacophony of life.
I am only ever certain of one thing,
In you I have the most understanding and truly magical wife.

Lee Tellis Adams

To You My Auburn Angel

Could it be? The segregated seraph laced me in her gaze?
This desolate mind is reimbursed, elated with enlustred rays.
When cast a' glimpse of auburn hair, the sun would beam in raucous stare.
Dishevelled in a coursing smile, though I see the scars encased within,
she shines a gleam of angel's tears, my mannequin of porcelain.
In admiration's mirrored pitch, I've captured your distinctive soul,
to fix and mould, then preach anew, the truer jewel amidst the coal.
Before my presence you'd lye bemused, with your thoughts distraught, forlorn.
Beyond completion you would stand the brightest rose amidst the thorns.
Why must you mask such unsurpassed visual revelry?
Internally I'm mesmerised by utterly embellished glee.
I catch your fall within my mind, signified, your light so true.
In my arms, solely encased, upon my touch I pledge to you.
Those aromatic fruits I taste, inside these sinuses erased,
to smell once more, when next we meet, and become as one with our
embrace.
The love was lost inside my past, implicitly my heart would rain,
alas with you, a love so true, I never thought I'd feel again . . .

Steven Kuhn

'Slow Down, Take Time'

Take your time is all I ask,
You keep ignoring my pleas.
I know you hear me,
You know that I'm right.
Please walk this path with me.

What is this race you're in?
Who are you racing against?
Wishing away time to get to the end,
Thinking the process quicker.
Take time and be in the moment,
As painful as that may be.

Slow down and breathe,
Deal with the now,
The future will just happen.
You're missing so much,
Not seeing the now,
Missing the full experience.

Live for the moment,
Walk this path with me,
Believe you can be free.
Breathe, relax, and take your time,
Repair your inner foundations.

The world will be waiting,
Full of love and acceptance,
To enjoy the new found you.
Be true to yourself, remember your worth,
What is rightfully yours will come.

My work with you must come to an end,
Me, an involuntarily redundant parent,
Fall back on memories, in moments of despair,
Never forget, time is always there.
Remember me fondly holding your hand,
As you explore this new land . . .

Suzanne Rawlinson

Spare

Now . . .
        choose a table by the window
        vantage point
        quick exit
        a newspaper
        pen for the crossword
        Cappuccino, no sugar
        a lemon muffin
        comfy clothes
        comfort food
        no calories, surely

Then . . .
        slim elegance opens the door
        followed by her brood
        blond, bookish, bobbed, little tribe
        joking, jostling to the counter
        leaning, reaching, demanding
        I want! I said it first!
        Marshmallows, muffins
        a lemon muffin, or two, or three
        Sit still! Share! Don't squabble!

Now . . .
        the wheels of time
        grind coffee slowly
        slow-release of lonely aromas
        cacophony of coffee breath all around
        contrasts the solitary customer
        her brood grown up
        and independent
        with busy lives
        'We'll call you soon!'

Now . . .
        slim elegance half turns
        catches the eye
        of comfy-clad middle-aged loneliness
        spare time to do a crossword?
        Strange to sit alone

in a crowded place
the gaze is met again
and for a brief second
each recognises the other

spare time
spare part
spare a thought . . .

Agnes Brookes

Love's Miracle Touch

Love, life's tantalising treasure,
Is safe where everyone can see
Yet it's without form or measure,
And free, with no safeguarding key.
Like faith it can't be bought or sold
To be spoiled by the cuckold.

Feeling your love's miracle touch
Sent my emotions all awhirl
For in you I'd met my nonesuch,
My dream one-in-a-million girl,
As I did twenty six years ago
When your kiss meant 'Yes' to this beau.

You were Heaven sent, I dare shout,
Of that none caring for us could doubt
As each joyful year led to more
Since your Engagement 'Yes' of yore
We etched on the Bridge at Dron
Deep into one wall's capping stone.

Ronald Rodger Caseby

Song Of The Mascarenes I-IV

I: The Hut

Barefoot and brown-legged, I drift across
sand and banana leaves to my secret spot
in the palm tree clearing. Light dapples,
creasing the view of Grandmother's house.

The breeze arouses the morning's sloth,
mingling with the damp scent of frangipani.
Here, I can shed my snake-skin; scales slip
noiselessly beneath the hut's timber planks

and I am a child again, eyeing green geckos
flick up prickling walls. I give each one
a name and a history, and a tiny forked soul.
Time is stubborn. I perch for hours, watching.

II: The House

Grandmother calls. As wrinkled as a lychee,
she takes my hand and sweeps me indoors.
The kitchen leans against the blazing frame of
a flame-tree, burnt red and gold in a heated haze.

Eat, eat the bread, she tells me, the soft dough
a cure for the ache in my belly which plagues
me nightly and wrenches me from sleep.
And I eat, feeling the white mass wrap around

my throat, watching crinkling eyes blink,
the toothless smile, the gentle trembling nod.
Does she know what I have become? I ease
out, glowing fiery, into the shameful, sultry heat.

III: The Sacrifice

For dinner we will have chicken. Grandmother
is in the yard, with its pungent smell of wet earth
and shit. She yammers at my uncle, faint traces
of a language I remember, and points to a hen,

fat, brown, bobbing vacuously about the soil,
oblivious. My brother retches at the sight of the
knife. Why can't it be quick? Instead, the blade
slices sleepily across the softly pulsing throat,

releasing an ooze of crimson glue which runs
sluggardly into the dust. The hen twitches, limp,
eyes cold marbles of emptiness. Grandmother
laughs at our heaving. We go hungry that night.

IV: Tamarind Falls

Past the Sugar Loaf Rock, petrified loneliness in
a turquoise vacuum, and a little way from the
Seven Coloured Earths, dusty fireworks forever
extinguished, lie Tamarind Falls. I boulder-hop

along the river bend, until the seven cascades
come into view. If I'm careful, and with time
to spare, I can reach the clear blue water at the
bottom of the force, a limpid living bath, calling

me back to life. Naked, I am witness to myself:
joyous and laughing, ripples of troubled conscience
slowly ebbing from my soul. The reeds coil like
emerald wires around my thighs. Soon I must go home.

Sarah Safraz

Memories

You danced with me
And only spoke a word or two
And I did not talk to you
We glided around the floor
And you walk away from me and out the door
I knew I would see you no more
You are just a memory
I have found someone that dances just like you
Used to do
I am no longer shy
This time he won't be
Walking out the door
I have forgotten you
You are no longer a memory

Joyce Margaret Sherwood

Our Relationship

How do I describe my relationship with you?
The world won't understand
The feeling when you take my hand
And flow
Effortlessly
The way you read my thoughts
And touch me intimately
The sensation you leave on my lips
Whispering secretly
Breathing rhythmically
My eyes close as I let you take charge
You reach deep into my soul
Lifting me up under the stars
The starry night above us
As the rain is racing down to Earth
But I'm indulged in you
Your eyes captivate me
I'm activated
When our minds collide
Combine
Fingers entwined
As we create fireworks in the sky
Making hearts pound
Sending shivers down their spine
They grab hold to the fabric of life
As we unfold a reality
Of this relationship that can't be described

As soon as we connect
They forget,
That this is an uncommon sight
You and me, it is unheard of
Considered absurd because we are of two different types
How can we go hand in hand?
You are assumed to be westernised
Whereas I am seen as a bird in backward flight
You glisten when they listen to you
The whole world rises at their feet
Left hands meeting right hands in a melody of victory
But when I stand at your side

They become uneasy
The atmosphere changes, it changes completely

But this is everything they forget when we connect
Because now when I stand with you
There are a million gazes looking up at me
Hands trembling I look upon faces of wonder
As they ponder upon their line of vision
We are a collision
But we don't create a dark night of meteorite destruction
We bring down a shower of diamonds executed to precision
I see faces of awe
Raised eyebrows of surprise
Nodding heads of acknowledgement
Smiles of support
Jaw-dropping mouths forming one word
Wow

I smell no fear
Emitting from sweaty palms of anxiousness
The scraping of chairs I don't hear
Of legs scuffling backwards
I feel their suspended silence
Backs arched forward
Eagerly awaiting
Fingernail biting
Maybe doubting
If I am successful
Hatred I don't taste
But the flavour of love embraces my taste buds
Because they understand now
That we fit together like two pieces of a jigsaw puzzle
That our bond isn't forbidden
Our secret doesn't have to be hidden
Right hands meet left hands in harmonious melody
This time not just for you but more for me
Showing that we are accepted, as one
A relationship that can't be described

You find me a cause for eruption
And I erupt
A volcano, spitting sense into the microphone
Hot lava melting

My character shedding off my skin
Dripping
You stand at the front line
You find me a mountain and I climb
Today, one step
Tomorrow, another step
Every day another trek
Till I reach the beacon of light
That's at the peak of this adventure that I embarked on with you
When we connect
They won't forget
They will always remember
Every time I reveal a new line of priceless treasure

They have witnessed
An uncommon sight
An uncommon experience
For I am a poet
And poetry is my intelligence

Aakifah Aboobakar

Writing Poetry – A Sonnet

How my heart is heavy with unspoken love,
And the passion poetry alone can prove.
'Til the song that sits in frustration's breast
descends on the page and grants me rest,
I must pay my tithe in sufferance.
Strange yet real comes the majesty in this,
The ailing artist begs for Aoidé's kiss
and the equal blessing of her siblings too
to be unchained and made a poet new.
Such is the way their disciples dance,
and would dance again, if given the chance.

Robert Smith

The Autumn Leaves Of Hell

The autumn leaves surround my feet,
They toss and swirl
In blood-red autumn hues
Of strong, inevitable decay.
The autumn mists are swirling
Round my head,
My heart cries out,
'You cannot leave!'

We met, and loved,
And filled our hearts with strong desire;
But duty calls,
It can't be missed,
And we must part.
But through the centuries of time
We'll search to find each other once again,
How many partings will we make?
How many journeys over land and sea?

You see my dear,
I loved too much,
And now you're gone,
And I must build again
A life in which you never were.
Welcome to Hell, in the autumn of the year.

Jane F Foster

Dance

Dawn cracks,
A new egg spilling red ribbons
Over the retired chimney stacks,

Tendrils riding on the minutes,
Curling around redbrick nests,
Sweeping under doorways,
Prancing through the curtains,

Still we slumber on,

Kings in our thrones, my love,
We don't need the nudge,
We wake with the tick
And rise with the tock,

Eyes now blurry and coffee now piping
We are the un-hearing audience
To the well-rehearsed song,

We disregard the dewy kisses
As splashes of the night
And stumble on our way,
To an office out of sight,

We plug in,
Switch on
And countdown the minutes,
To repeat the journey,
Rewinding our steps,

Stars blanket the city,
As we turn in,
We turn off
And we reclaim our thrones,

We are not the kings,
We thought we once were,
Play your sweet music,
Oh, choir sing louder!
We are your dancers,
It is your lead that we take,

Look up -
My love, where are you going?
Look up -
My love, you are missing the show.

Charlotte Chase

Theo The Cat With The Question Mark Tail

Theo the cat with the question mark tail
Went to sea to see a whale
With his question mark tail
He could not hide
So he saw the whale . . . but from the inside.

Theo the cat with the question mark tail
Wandered curiously inside the whale
Tickled its tonsils 'til out of its throat
Theo was sneezed
Right into a boat

Theo the cat with the question mark tail
Became famous for being inside a whale
He travelled the world
Saying this, saying that
Theo became a very homesick cat.

Theo the cat with the question mark tail
Went to the sea and called the whale.
Who took him back home to his fireside chair
Where he sits with his tail
Curled round his ear

Mary L

Transition

The idle birds have run their course;
They fly to some bitter-sweet memory
Alone in the shadows of wondrous days
Harmony and peace were one
Flowers as bright as jewels and distorted
Upon a child-like mind in my days gone
Happiness was wading through snow
Never noticing the cold and frozen air
Love was simplistic – hearts of gold
Unconditional with a flicker of light
How times have changed
Love is for the weak and blind
Happiness of better times to come
Fictional stories were only that
Maybe a glimpse into a faraway world
The flowers became lifeless
The snow a burden on the soul

Once touched – never forgotten or forgiven
Only once and the birds fly away
Only once and we are changed for eternity
The innocence thrust upon us at birth
Regret is that of a larger nature
As time ticks away the list grows further
Though one memory stands above all
Touch; all it takes
Wrong places or time for the doing of good
If I had lived for myself, no regrets would I have
We aim to please others before ourselves
Consequences are merely a thought
Banished; away from reality
Until the fall of all good, if that can be named
Repetition of regret, with every second that passes
Tolerated in the moment, for another as we do
Then realise the damage within the mind
Time does not go backwards
Cannot undo the past in its place
Like a scar on the brain – or heart if so
I am reminded of those times
Only giving what we thought we must give

To receive what we deserved to receive
Until realising the regret in plain day
To have the birds back
Or any other of its nature
Too far from reach but a memory of the past
Remaining in light, never to be seen

Georgia Head

Alive

I awake as a new winter dawn appears. The room feels colder than the season and is deathly quiet. I glance at the clock. It is blank. A power cut? I'm surprised as I did not hear a storm last night but it's not unusual in this remote cottage?

In the half light I tread my way carefully to the bathroom. The necessary done I feel the need for a warm drink before my shower. I go downstairs to the kitchen and try to light the gas hob. No gas. No water in the tap. I look around the brightening room with mild consternation. The wall clock has stopped. It can't possibly be three am or pm.

No power! The fridge. Oh no! I open the door expecting to find room temperature milk but it is completely solid and the plastic has decomposed. A lump of meat has mummified. I can't identify the rest of the desiccated contents.

Alarmed I run upstairs to wake my husband. I shout his name as I reach the bedroom but he does not respond. I shout again but he must be fast asleep under the duvet. I garble on about the clock, the fridge, the power cut and the cold. Whilst pacing about I open the curtains and say, 'Peter! Are you awake?' I go up to him and in the now bright room I scream and scream as I am confronted by a long since decomposed and mummified skeleton!
The children!

Margaret Edge

Burnished? Tarnished? You Decide

I have always managed to start afresh,
And never looked to keep in touch.
Maybe it helps, but I don't really know,
Do others find they need a crutch.

At times I can be down and low,
But then she comes around to brighten the day.
I have no time to think of broken dreams,
Her constant chatter and awesome looks,
Drive all of my cares away.

I wonder about 'Friends and Foes' from early life,
Would they still have some appeal.
The town where I was born and raised,
Is built and formed on 'Steel'.

'The Manor', sounds a nice place to live,
It was built to house, the many, not the few.
The 'Edge' of town wasn't much better,
But at least it was green and new.

I will not linger, long, on school,
'Roman Catholic', you see.
When I wasn't fighting off bigger kids,
'The Devil's Guard' beat the crap out of me.

Then I served an apprenticeship,
To work as a skilled and managed 'Tool'.
Till signs went up, 'This town for sale or rent'.
But we can, re-train 'The Fool'.

We have since become wiser better men,
Taken on skills that are 'New'.
Resurrected from 'Iron, Steel and Coal'.
But at least, we smell better, in the 'Queue'.

My life has gone on, in fits and starts,
But still it has more ups than downs.
Will it have one more 'Twist', who knows.
'Bring on the Clowns'.

So I wait for her to come round, once more,
To smile and bring in the light.
And with her, a 'Stainless Heart'

As mine is 'Hammered', 'Black as Night'.

Epilogue
Some may find religion gives them strength,
To conquer there doubts and fears.
But all it ever did for me my friend,
Is scar me for years and years.

Sheffphil

The Last Train

He held on tight, soaking wet. A train sped past.

A dog with a bone; you know the type, just won't let go.

He *couldn't* let go. Why had she refused him?

Joe had it all; good looks, house, fast car, money. What's not to like? Yet she'd refused him.

If you turn up on the doorstep of your girl's house, dressed in Armani, brandishing a bouquet of velvet-red roses, how can she resist? You don the winning smile, make a fool of yourself on one knee, gaze up with doleful eyes and say, 'Marry me!' Then, in front of the curtain-twitching neighbours, she says no.

Well he'd show her, tell her what he was going to do. Then she'd change her mind and come running. He'd sent a text repeating his proposal; she was working and it remained unread. That was the final straw.

In the torrential rain, the bridge railings were slippery. His grip weakened. A second train rattled the metal beneath his hands. Maybe he didn't really want to do this. A crowd had gathered on the grass far below. Was she there?

How to get back up to the track, though? One foot found a broad girder. His strong arms pulled up, his feet found further purchase and up he went. The crowd cheered. Then started waving. He wondered why. Only at the last second did he realise. A third train thundered down as he stood on the track.

Frances Marshall

May I?

May I walk with you, may I understand
May I stand with you, may I take your hand
May I see the light that others asininely demand
May someone guide me, may I one day aspire
May I talk with you, may I stand on common ground
May I cross that divide that bigotry solemnly commands
May I call you my friend, may I hold you in my arms
May I lay my weapon down
                    May I?

Ian Street

The Affair

So hard to say goodbye after so many years
As we bid our farewell, let's part without tears
I thought we were solid, and never apart
We relied on each other from an early start
So how could such bonding be put asunder this way
How could we decide that just one of us stay?
We've been together now for fifty-two years
To split at this moment could trigger such fears
Yet split we must action if we're to survive
And live for the future and not family deprive
So farewell my fags, my lighter, cigars
You're history now though I still bear the scars
But now I don't need you for me there's no scare
I have to declare now I end the affair

Graham Hayden

Lost Labour

This time yesterday, designer suits, efficiency and management systems were my trademark. Today, I am on the sofa cocooned in the duvet, wide screen flickering, sound muted. Through half closed plantation blinds, life continues. The disposal of the detritus of better times is nosily snatched and crushed, so as not to taint our landscaped vista.

I didn't tell Mike when he skyped; long distance may as well be Mars, where there are no lexicons to express disappointment. Thankfully, the scrambled screen did not betray my swollen eyes… besides, I didn't want him to lose focus.

Mike's good morning text read… 'Mission accomplished! Big Bonus! I'm the Daddy!! CU soon J'.

The words pierced me, even in their concise form.

Here, in the designer lounge of my dreams, the clock's staccato tick stabs in small incisions… a repetitive, torturous execution.

In half an hour, the quiet hum of our Lexus will turn onto the drive… a symbol of our prosperity. We had such plans… perfect timing, exemplary nutrition...

He was astrologically divined for God's sake… god… that's a joke. Our scan had been a lesson in unconditional love and unexpressed parental desire; he had Mike's nose and my vitality… *had*… it all…

Today's forecast is sunshine and showers; a cruel reminder that rainbows are mere tricks of the light.

My Armani work coat is on the parquet floor where it fell last night, the 'Baby on Board' badge now… surplus to requirements.

Laura Annansingh

I've Fallen In Love With Mr Muscle!

The typical skittish behaviour when my body begins to bustle
All in the fact that I've fallen in love with the one and only Mr Muscle
How his passionate vibe shines when cleaning down my decks
As his toned, articulate physique moves, rhythmical with his pecs!

I absolutely idolise his devotedness to cleaning; his pure dedication
I never knew in a million years, I'd fall at the feet of a fictional animation
Every time he appears on the telly, he sends me into an ultimate lust of
dreaming
Of his hard grafting work of solving solutions, the master scientist of cleaning!

Everybody reckons I'm 'crazy' when I tell them that someday he'll save my fate
He's the heroic figure that loves the jobs that I certainly hate
You can rely on his problematic fixtures, you can abide by his terms
You can depend on his assurance when he says he can kill your unwanted
toilet germs!

He assassinates those horrid spiders, he knows they drive me insane
He's the superhero with the professional touch of unclogging my crummy
drain
He knows how to abide in a woman's animosity, when her hygiene's repelling
hell
He knows how to retrieve the optimism with his magical bathroom gel!

So divorce your apathetic husband sisters; upgrade to a supreme
Man that can harbour the pressure and contain a vigorous hygiene
Experience the typical skittish behaviour when my body begins to bustle
All in the fact that I've fallen in love with the one and only Mr Muscle!

Jamie H Scrutton

Wildflowers

I love the beautiful wildflowers that people call weeds
They can be seen everywhere as most of them self-seed
There are thousands of wildflowers if only their names I knew
But could not begin to remember them all so here are a few.

They come up in all sorts of places your grass and flower beds
Like the dandelion, one which I love with its golden head
The nettle with its leaf that stings, the cowslip and primrose
You see them when out, growing at the side of the roads
The yarrow with its flower of white or could be a lovely yellow
And the golden sunny buttercup that everyone will know
The red, white or pink clover with leaves that are three or four
Just wish I could know all their names as so many more
So here are some more I expect most of you might know
The ones that come up in our gardens, but lots of places they grow
Cornflower, and the forget-me-not, my favourite colour of blue
And the tall white daisy flower that is called feverfew
Poppy, bluebell, fennel, chickweed, pansy, marigold and milk thistle
Wallflower, love-in-a-mist, daffodil, wildrose, violet and that is not all.

There is just one more to mention before I go, this is the last
Is the sweet pretty white daisy that's always on our grass
All the insects, butterflies love them, and so do the bees
Like me please see them as beautiful wildflowers not just weeds . . .

Lindy Roberts

Spray Attack

Living her insular life -
The desperate author,
put pen to paper,
one more time
embellished the blank page
with desperate words
of deep despair.

The latest attack
came without warning
without hope of preparation.
A busy fashion store
the location.

Spray . . .
directed at the tender
facial skin and eyes -
the stinging sensation
came first -
then the burning.
As eyelids closed
to protest against any
further assault
on the delicate tissue.

Shock horror.

As the face of the attacker
came into view.
Holding up a mobile phone
to capture the victim's reaction
on camera.

*A dark evil
closes in.*

The traumatised woman
crying out for help -
desperate eyes
searched for an assistant -
anyone.

*Help
seemed non-existent.*

Eyes now filled with tears
like a fast-flowing river
they ran . . .
could not be stemmed.

The taste of salt
on her lips now,
swelling, by the second.

Other shoppers, pushing her -
reached over
as the traumatised victim
became invisible.

Beautiful clothing
trampled underfoot
a stampede almost.
The terrified woman
crying out -
for *help.*

The hottest day
of the year -
yet the coldness of people.
Impossible to understand
leaving the hunted woman
to run . . .
for her life.

Out into the street -
a 'sea' of unknown faces.
The burning sensation
spreading, like a virus
across her face.

The deeply traumatised woman -
speaking out loud now -
'Got to get home,
got to get home.'

Caught up in a maelstrom
of *terror*
without thought
without reason
without *hope.*

Nina Graham

Helmsley Walled Garden

I saw it last weekend
In a way not seen before
From above
An aerial description from a helicopter
During the Tour de France
Enclosed, wrapped up in glorious boundaries

I have usually visited in summer
The first time was before lunch
I marvelled at the view
And took photographs of the abundant species of flowers

A sensory perception
Audible sounds of distant sheep
And the low soft hum of bees
Mixed with delightful aromas
Of the scents
of myriads of flowers

Random gardening equipment
hinted at the upkeep, toil and history
the presence of caretakers,
the many different colours
at different heights
Painting by number delight

Catherine Lynne Kirkby

VJ Day (1945)

And where were you on VJ Day?
With festive joy in London's streets;
Bunched tightly in Trafalgar Square?
Or did you stay indoors and silent weep
For those who never could again be there.

Perhaps you ran to fill The Mall
And sing and dance and swap a kiss?
For all the world seems to be gathered there
To share this moment of euphoric bliss.

Or were you with the ghosts along the track
Of that steel murder trail in Burma's heart?
With gnarled and battered body torn apart;
Hungrily hoping with tortured mind
In fetid squalor, still groping to find
Some sense in living. Clinging
Wildly onto dreams,
Clinging onto hope,
Clinging onto life -
Just.
Wildly clinging!
Can there be a God out there?
Is there singing,
Still, somewhere?

For whom are the church bells ringing?
For the joy of Mankind in victory air?

Or do they toll for the man-made hell
That we as men create so well
Whilst blaming God for all our pain?
No. They warn us of war that will come again.

Donald Wood

As She Thought Of You

As she lay in bed with a guy,
A year younger than her,
Naked,
Bodies entwined,
Stroking his hair,
Both filled with warmth and joy,
She thought of you

Feeling satisfied,
The body never lying,
Yet the heart beating behind her ribcage was,
Her mind in a daze,
Guilt washed over her,
Catching her between reality and dream,
As she thought of you

She wanted to be loyal to you,
But she knew it would do no good,
The temptation was too great,
He gave her an easy way out,
Of her miserable dwelling,
As she thought of you

Back in her life you came,
Just as quickly as when you left,
Still embedded in her memory,
The promises you made,
Sweet nothings,
Held within her wall of hope,
Her mind and heart beating fast,
Oh the growing lust,
The excitement,
As she thought of you

Your brown eyes met her own,
Hers darker in shade,
Strong too,
Her smile takes you a-back,
Humble and caring,
The girl who stood before you,
Full of love and warmth,
Friendship,

Like the pictures you would look at,
You remember her,
(As she thought of you)

Sara Nadeen Ashbourne

Shadow Dancing

To secret places I am led
by dancing shadows on my shed.

The sun shines through the leafy trees
all swaying in the whispering breeze
they're forming shapes and pirouettes
and prancing, dancing silhouettes.

Despite the quiet of the day
there's music where the shadows play
and while I doze in my deckchair
unspoken lyrics fill the air.
Yes! Melodies are all around
my feet are firmly on the ground
but when the shadows interweave
I'm in a world of make-believe.

I'm dancing as the shadow's tune
pervades the lazy afternoon
but though I saunter, full of zest
the neighbours see a man at rest.

At night-time, when I go to bed
those dancing shadows fill my head.

Jonathan Bryant

Angler's Blues

I woke up this morning, it was gloomy and grey,
Went down to the river, as usual on a Sunday,
Walked on down to the bend, then over the bridge,
Poured a tea from my flask, chewed a cheese sandwich.

From the case comes the rod, then a reel and some line,
There's a break in the clouds, will there be some sunshine?
Tied on a new hook, some lead weights, and a float,
What's this I perceive! There's some fool in a boat!

Well, now he's out of the way, I can now settle down,
At last some peace and quiet, far away from the town,
Baiting up with some maggots, throw in a few from the tub,
Just to get the shoals feeding, the roach, dace and chub.

Casting into the swim, keeping my eyes on the quill,
Making no sound at all, and keeping perfectly still,
With a dip it goes down, and a flick of the wrist,
Have I go this one? Yes? No! Dammit I've missed!

A juicy worm on the barb, maybe a barbel will bite,
A mighty swirl in the water, and one hell of a fight!
A gust of wind catches the line, it ends up in a tree,
And try as I may, I just cannot get it free!

After much pulling and tugging, there's eventually a crack,
And what's left of the tackle, comes drifting on back,
Think I'll try with a ledger, and maybe a crust of bread,
What's happening now! Well, this is something I dread!

It's a couple of swans, and with them their brood,
Swimming down with the current, on a search for some food,
Followed from behind, by some geese and a duck,
This sure isn't my day; it's just my kind of luck!

Things must surely get better, can't get any worse!
Will I always be jinxed, or am I touched by a curse!
Try again in deeper water, in the slack of the stream,
Keep my eye on the rod tip, hope for a nice big bronze bream!

With a twitch of my pole, well time strike, and I've hooked,
Reaching for my net, this old fish sure is spooked!
My heartbeat is racing, I start to feel my feet sink,
As I slide down the bank, and fall headlong into the drink!

Scrambling out of the water, I say enough is enough!
The sky is dark, the heavens open, it's sure turning rough,
I'm coughing and sneezing, boy, am I feeling meek,
But I'll be back again, same time, same place, next week!

Geoff Cook

Nearly Nine

There's a golden haired maiden,
By the name of Marnie French.
She's as pretty as a picture,
Such a perfect little wench.

She's a darling, she's an angel,
She's a devil in disguise.
And as you might have guessed by now,
She's the one I idolise.

She likes lollipops and bubblegum,
We call her the bubble queen.
And she blows the biggest bubbles,
That your eyes have ever seen.

She likes animals and potato crisps,
Likes dressing up her dolls.
Likes muddy pools and make-up,
And wearing noisy Scholes.

She sings out loud and clearly,
All funny songs that rhyme.
She likes handstands, non-stop dancing,
And she giggles all the time.

She fills my hours with so much fun,
This little girl of mine
Who's nearly nine.

Lara Day

Lest I Forget

Death did not claim William
On the beaches at Dunkirk,
It looked away, its rheumy eyes
Searching the future in a far-off land
Where prayers could be heard.

But, providence had found its muse,
Came masquerading as the benefactor
Of William's good fortune while
Hiding its fickle nature under
A thin veil of benevolence.

William was sent to Singapore.
Fate – not wishing to be tempted
A second time turned against him.
Unravelled by his own tenacity
He met his nemesis on the
Burma Railway.

Death did not claim William
On the beaches at Dunkirk,
It looked away, and found him
Praying in a far-off land
For liberation that took too long
And came too late.

William Woodcock
1920-1944
Beloved son, brother and uncle.

Linda Woodcock

Death Of A Rebel

I know you loved me
You loved the rebel
For I was James Dean, and your Clark Gable
Your fantasy. Your action hero
Your Errol Flynn, sweet Valentino
You smiled and laughed, the silence so loud
Funny like Chaplin, king to your clowns
That lovable rogue, protector and foe
I was Godfather babe, your Marlon Brando
I'd played every part, you know wasn't easy
Those tragic scenes, you saw without screaming
There stood a man, full of hunger and greed
Just being myself, meant a life on my knees
We took to the road, you hijacked my life
It was fun while it lasted
We were Bonnie and Clyde

Deadboy

Blossom

I want the flowers and the trees' sway
all rolled up, as we are, blossom
to blossom, heat to heat, scent
to scent. Petals and leaves scrunched,
beauty all compact. Weeks of autumn,

Spent amongst each other, colours
too vibrant to explain, careless
and carefree. Let the winter come,
we have faced it before; it didn't
take our blossom, heat, or scent.

Jos. Connor Hepplestone

Time Please

I suppose you never stop missing it, will never stop missing, it.
That bouncing foaming amber as it hits the bottom of the five o'clock held
iced glass.
No, I'm not trying to look down the armpit of your blouse love.
I'm just watching to see you're pouring it right.
Easy on the gas but hurry up for God's sake.
The pop of that wine cork.
Christ these glasses are small now me mates have got married,
mortgaged their souls and think they've joined the ranks of the middle-class.
But I know in a multiple choice test he'd still option etiquette as part of the
three-day event.
I remember him decapitating a bottle on the pavement outside the Forum
and spitting out the splinters of glass, before cracking that front tooth playing
mental macho on a metal bottle top.
And tell her we're not in a restaurant; she can fill the glasses up,
no one's looking, it's not a tasting session.
And are there another half a dozen bottles in the fridge?
All the supermarkets do three for two these days
and you're both earning a few quid off the council for doing very little.
And did you get some red as well?
I don't really give a toss what colour the meat is, as long as white booze is
chilled,
red's been allowed to breathe and there's a bottle of Napoleon or Malt, or
maybe both to wash everything down with.

But all that clinical talk of sperm counts, the most effective time of the day and
babies strangles my libido.
So I'm off to the City where they really know how to party;
munch schemie Es like kids over the pick 'n' mix,
down pints with double voddie Red Bull chasers
and race relay to the gents for lines of Conquistador's marching powder.
Then rocking the Casbah,
even if the kids on the dance floor do think a dad's turned up to collect a
curfewed child and been slipped a Mickey Finn.
A couple of hours of snoring behind the settee before the legendary Leith
Breakfast,
the World's best and most generous Bloody Mary; with tabasco, worcester
sauce, white pepper, celery salt and a squeeze of lemon.
Back to the pub for seven or eight gentle pints and a blether about the night's
misdemeanours before standing freezin' our b******s off watching the next

pathetic shower being trotted out onto hallowed ground on free transfers in your beloved green.

Where do you get them from? That geezer couldn't get in Chelsea's under twelves.

God it's tatters up here.

Look I'll meet you in the pub when this shite finishes.

Why do bad football matches always seem to last twice as long?

Yes, I'll have some whiskies lined up for you all when you get there.

Oxford says abstinence is: 'the act of abstaining'.

It doesn't feel like an act, it feels f****n' real enough to me.

And you were right mate:

Denial is not just a river in Egypt and De Niro is never gunna be as good as he used to be.

It's time to put the brakes on.

Too many pals have checked out.

You included.

I'm at a crossroads, where one fork leads straight over Beachy Head and I'm scared of the height.

I peered over when I was a kid.

My mother still sends me a calendar of it every New Year,

as if seven sisters were my collective lost loves, instead of knowing they're my biggest fear.

So for now, not for me the park bench,

anything alcoholic in hand,

anyone who'll listen at my side, as long as I'm buying.

A fellow lost soul to chew the bones of life's injustices.

Time for a rain check

and maybe

to build some bridges

if there's time left

before the bell.

Alan Harman

Steam

A black beat sways across the battered bar,
Causing tales and formidable ice cubes
To burst forth before face-painted fools,
Who gossip and gallivant about a star
Until someone walks away.

Timeless glass spirals over a pub with no purpose,
Where bloody liars and lovers rave to blues
And rage to keep at bay their worldly feuds.
The club owner at the door says, 'He's the boss,'
But he's not the one who fuels glasses to fumigate souls.

Automatic, catastrophic cars with static radios arrive,
And in come statues with their feet in satellite-high heels;
Start dancing under globes of pink, forgetting their deals,
They play games with rays of light and steam to stay alive.
The world is neither dead nor alive – it's filled with three grey hues.

Gemma Morrish-Williams

In Memory

One hundred years ago this year
Men from our village marched out with a cheer
With brave smiling faces, and thoughts of those dear
They marched out to war without any fear.

But when it was over we counted the cost
Few came back but many were lost
They'd laid down their lives so we could have peace
They gave it willingly for all wars to cease.

The peace we had was not to last
Another war loomed its mighty blast
Our men went out again to fight
For freedom speech and all that's right.

There is no greater love than this
When many gave their lives defending us
So we've put up this monument for all to see
We remember those who died for our country.

Joan Littlehales

The Soul Well

I am smoke
vapour in stone throat
I don't move, I do nothing but wait.
Overhead I see cold stars
in dark night sky, moving like lights.
Sometimes, I sing songs.
I am mist and moonlight
my memory is sad, old.
Sometimes I fall like rain
spiderwebs are startled
into forming where my rain falls
on water's surface.
I wait in cool silence.
Now it is morning, I listen,
I hear voices far away:
I hang like golden pollen on airy breeze
invisible, misting in light.
A voice.
I turn in sun, a wheel
endlessly spinning out my life.
Water ripples, I rise in warm air,
a shadow looms before me -
water. Pure and sweet, soft wind.
I listen to the sounds of voices
I do not understand, their words form
like water on a tongue, falling
with slow beauty out of air,
I rise, as in a cool well, released.
A face above me, water ripples,
a stone drops into me.
Sun dies. Stars wheel upon night sky.

I am a soul well.
I wait here, I listen to wind's sound.
I am smoke, I draw thoughts from those
who drink vapour from my throat
I am soul well, come and drink from me.

Teta

Great British TV Commercials

In the UK, we have to pay our licence fee for watching TV
If we're under the age of seventy-five
But the only reason why we pay it is to fund the BBC
And we can also be exempt if we're blind
Many channels fund themselves by showing ads
Commercials for food, other products and the latest fads
Commercials for soap or toothpaste, bicycles or cars
Adverts for cereals, mashed spuds or a chocolate bar called Mars
Which supposedly helps you 'work, rest and play'
If you partake of it on a daily basis, or so they say
And do you recall those green blobs that fell across the screen
In the ads for a medicated shampoo called Vosene?
There was one that said it was 'good for mums'
And showed a boy getting shampooed in the bath, sitting on his bum
Did you used to clean your kitchen floor with Flash?
Maybe you got the idea to do this from TV
As we were assured that it 'Cleans floors fast',
Quickly getting them spotless for all visitors to see
Adverts can also launch the careers of bands
Whether you think their music is exciting, raucous or bland
Some of them can also make us more safety conscious
As we wouldn't wish to end up dead or unconscious
Colgate toothpaste was advertised to the tune of a Madness song
And ads for air fresheners showed us what could rid our homes of pongs
There have been adverts on our TV screens since 1955
That was before the days of 'Coronation Street', 'Top of the Pops', or Channel 5
Ads for a drink called Martini – 'Anytime, anywhere, any place'
Adverts for the latest movies where they're travelling out in space
So perhaps your favourite ice cream, custard or soft drink
Was one you initially saw advertised on the box
And it was that very commercial which made you start to think;
'Wow – I must get some of that stuff – it rocks!'

Philip Dalton

For Bronya

Pitch sky rent by lightning.
An ancient doctrine shattered by courage.
A promise vase, dropped with a yell of destruction.

The firmament glues back together, zipped up.
The archaic belief is uprooted, a new tradition sown.
But the promise vase lies shattered, its essence gone.

Shards of porcelain lodge daily in the foot.
A subtle, painful, just punishment.
A frantic hunt begins for scattered pieces,
eyes straining for a glimpse of a world containing reconstructing.

Some pieces thrown away,
some pieces lost.
Some pieces returned by friends and strangers,
some pieces so small they became part of the everything.

And then, relief flowing, in time segments reconnect.
From the base a signature emerges,
a 200-year-old connection.
Pastoral scenes reappear.
Pieces too hastily reglued timber again
producing yet more shards.

Until
a different vase emerges
and is finally
accepted
back.

Claire Robey

You Still Hold The Power

Staring into your black cold eyes,
Windows into the darkness of your soul,
I can see the real you.
You try to hide it but I still see.
You try to fool us all,
But I know what you've done.
It's written on your face,
And on the scars you've caused.

Your rotten smile tries to deceive us,
But the kindness is not real,
We do not believe it.
But why is it you have all the power?
Still controlling all our lives,
Your dirty hands still clutching on,
And pulling at our strings.
Trapped here by a higher power,
Who we cannot leave behind.

Cotton wool covering her eyes,
She still believes your lies.
Even after it all,
You control her heart ,
And her mind won't see.
Letting you play games,
Hurting the guiltless,
Unable to protect themselves.

The wounds you've caused run deep,
And cannot be erased.
They cannot be forgotten,
The past is in the past,
But it always finds a way.
To come back to the surface,
And hurt us all again.

Hannah Gibson

Goodnight Grandad

The main man in my life; that was you,
every situation, you knew what to do.
Only the best advice you would give,
you showed me the life I wanted to live.

You stood in my corner and helped me fight,
you stayed with me till they saw we were right.
Grandad and Granddaughter; what a team we became,
and I promise you one thing . . . we will meet again.

You went through so much; day after day,
but you never let the pain show in any way.
The strength you showed, it taught me a lot,
to stand for what's right and not move from that spot.

In my life you played a special part,
the memories I treasure and keep close to my heart.
You are my rock, my hero, my guide,
and in those last days, I hated leaving your side.

You gave it your all, till you could take no more,
then along came Heaven knocking at the door.
One last breath with a smile on your face,
we knew then you had reached your resting place.

Although you have gone; we will always be together,
and your spirit will live on in each of us forever.
You were really one in a million; a cut above the rest,
all that knew you would agree; you're simply the best.

The pain we feel now will hopefully fade,
and now comes the time; to rest you are laid.
I miss you Grandad, but enjoy where you are,
out of pain now forever, up with the stars.

In our thoughts you remain for evermore,
even though recent events feel so raw.
We love you so much but know why you left,
it's true what they say; they only take the best.

Charlotte Jeans

On A Mission

Can you stand out
And then fall in?
Blink and you miss it
That sparkle which is
A thirst for life
And learning.
Cocooned in a room
An institution that
You've outgrown,
But kept under wraps
Until you're ready
To roam free in your
Glorious butterfly form.
Preparing to stand out
And sparkle once more.

Susannah Cassidy

Cherry

Gentlemen, in velvet suits consumed without thought;
not a trace left on their hands.

You crawled to the table's edge and demanded to try one, but they all knew
you as a child and laughed as you tentatively tasted.

You just wanted the outside.
Children only ever want chocolate.

A drop of bitter cherry seeped through and you knew that inside there was –
a swilling in that sea, a child drowning in the ground.

So, you took it back from your mouth.
Strands of saliva, left hanging
and now, sweetheart, your hands are grubby.

Placing it in the fire it burnt blue.
You watched it; only then did you think it was pretty.

Holly Platt-Higgins

Inward Sorting – All Sections (Circa 1980)

The delivery lorry arrives plugged full of bags. Letter bags piled high, 'cause the wicker skips to creak loudly. Their wheels squeak repeatedly, perhaps in protest,
when pushed across the floor. Letter bag label strings are cut. Bundles tumbled into narrow standing troughs.

'Inward sorting… all sections'… now called across the floor.

Packets are poured into concertina expanders, that sink ever lower. Sorters stand either side to lob packets into named or numbered bags. Brick-like wads of phone bills, in high relief, stand in wicker troughs. First Class stamped and required delivery today.
Any early morning jollity… dampened by this mountain sight of letters, for delivery to every household on the walks today. A voice calls out in the midst -

'Sort and talk, sort and talk.'

- For those who've stopped to chat, and are no longer sorting while they're talking. A pressure storm of letters later slows momentum.

'Rural postmen, give us five minutes.'

Early rural postmen are called back to assist. Finally the last letter bundle is separated into several pairs of hands. The main frame then stripped of letters for each and every walk.

Quiet descends and letters melt from desk to frame with fluency. Now each experienced with his or her own delivery. Finally streets and destinations are desk ordered and bundle tied. The rural postmen place letter bundles in trays for their easy access. The town walk postmen stack lay their delivery into canvas pouches.

Sam Grant

Living Ghost

In my dreams every night there's a path that I follow,
Repetition's the road that I walk with eyes hollow
There's a house where I go, a slave to my slumber
This house I don't know, not the street nor the number
It happened just once as I grew over time
This dream left me haunted without reason or rhyme
Yet I learnt to forget and continue in life
Yet the torment returned when I became a wife
It begins as though I have no control
Placed involuntarily in this unwanted role
I look straight ahead to a hall not my own
Wallpaper, floorboards, the old-fashioned phone
All so familiar I know them, I know every part
This house that's not mine yet belongs in my heart
Turn left through the door and then right for the stairs
Every detail is mine to the box of éclairs
I walk up the stairs just like each night before
It's becoming a yearning, a need to see more
I wonder tonight, will the woman be there?
Whose eyes fill with fear as I turn to her chair
And those eyes when they see me, they know me, but how?
With her white golden hair and the sweat in her brow.
Every night I awake before I see any more
Before I've finished my walk, completed the tour
The blue door at the front and the windows antique
The walk down the drive to the porch with wood weak,
I go the same way walking down the same street
As though an internal compass has hold of my feet.
This picket fence house down this suburban lane
Each time I walk down all I can feel is pain
Where am I? What is this? Can someone please say.
When I wake in the morning why does it never stay?
I stop the car with such sorrow that I've never felt,
A quick glance in the mirror then I undo my belt,
Step out, walk around, figure out just exactly where am I
It is night-time already, there's no sun in the sky.
I turn round the corner, feet moving without me,
My consciousness absent like a drone worker bee,
Until I reach a house, blue door, faded paint

Reality smacks me, I begin to feel faint.
Just like in the dream I open the gate,
Not knowing, not caring the hour is late
My feet keep on moving until I reach the door
I knock, then I swallow, afraid to see more
Is this really happening? Am I actually here?
The pull is magnetic it makes me inch ever near
A woman answers, a woman I know
'No, no it can't be.' Her hair white as snow,
She falls in the porch affront that blue wooden door
And I follow after, my presence no more.

Holly Sturdy-Clow

For The Third Time

You tempt me with your clear cool water
on this hot August day
and I step into the crystal blueness
and feel myself sinking,
submerging in the swirling depth.

Am I safe though in such deep water?
Can I be sure you understand me?
I do not swim and I will not float
I walk towards you
my feet no longer touch the bottom.

You've told me that you love me,
that you wish me no harm
but your intensity is pulling at me
and your passion feels so heavy
like boulders weighing me down.

You are drawing me under
as I am grasping for the surface,
Through the water I see your face,
Smiling, yet filled with angst,
And I know I am drowned.

Ann Biggins

The Demon Within

In my head there is only confusion
The feeling I'm living my own delusion
An anger that sits in my heart's black hole
That will hurt those I love if I lose control

Simple things start it, if you're unaware
And often not justified just to be fair
Things others would not give a second thought
In my head are the signs that a war must be fought

Paranoid thoughts obsess my mind
Unjust? Unfair? And plain unkind
While those that have triggered it must never know
The lengths of revenge I'll have plotted to go

Those that are 'normal' would not comprehend
The strength of the rage that I have to keep penned
Uncertainty triggers it, I am aware
But those that surround me most likely don't care

It will pass, I am certain but could take its time
Meanwhile I must struggle to hold it in line
Can't speak without thinking, daren't relax my mind
Or all that I love will leave me behind

So I'm quiet, I will shun you, it's kinder to do
Than to show you the world from my point of view
You won't understand, think I'm taking the p**s
But I'm trying my best to protect you from this

It makes me a demon, there's no other word
And who needs that shit to descend in their world
And who could I blame for them running away
Were I them I also would not want to stay

For all of my life I have fought to control
This god awful darkness that eats up my soul
I'm strong, I'm a fighter I cannot give in
To the beast living in me, the devil within.

Maria Cummins

Thinking Too Much!

Yes, some of us, do think way too much!
Could be a hindrance, could be a crutch?
A date isn't as simple as some may think.
Does one wear blue or one wear pink?

First impressions count, so what to wear?
Everything's important, down to clothes and hair.
But feeling comfortable and being at ease.
Not having shaky hands or wobbly knees .

Arriving early, or maybe five minutes late.
All counts when meeting on a first date.
Sat waiting and watching, feeling like a spy.
Wondering if they see you, will they drive by.

Turning up late, you haven't got a clue.
What they are thinking, when they see you?
At that point, it is often too late to worry.
Maybe they will drive off, in a mad scary hurry?

That first hello, when the eye contact is made.
They wonder which one of them, feels most afraid?
A shake of hands, a friendly hug, a polite hello.
Neither of them knowing which way it will go?

It's all guess work, that first ten minutes meet.
Do you look into their eyes, or down at your feet?
Talk of family life, you're really not that sure?
Or past history, relationships, that could be a bore?

It's probably best, to just be yourself?
No one wants to hear, why you're now on the shelf?
Enjoy the moment and the experience of it all!
Try to be patient and wait to see if you get a call.

It may not happen, you may not want to hear again.
But if you do, you will want to know where and when?
It could be the start of something good or bad?
But you would never have known, until that first date you'd had?

Millie Barlow

In The Shadow Of Sophia

We thought we knew where we were going.
Heading east, we said,
not west.

We thought to chase the rising sun
and being young,
in present tense,
we ran in opposition
to the western shadow lengthening;
pulling black behind us,
trailing ignorance.

In time, Sophia cast herself
across our narrow path,
sewing pearls to silver ribbons
to reflect
the setting sun.

She wondered would we learn
to braid our days with iridescence,
considering the endless pebbles
birthing underfoot

or would we disregard ephemera,
refusing eyes the sense
to see how time and tense collide
in every tick-tock trickling
of pulse.

Laura Taylor

Who Killed John Lennon?

'Who killed John Lennon?' 'I' said Mark Chapman
'With my Smith and Wesson, I killed John Lennon.'
'Who saw him die?' 'Lucy in the sky,
From way up on high, she saw him die.'
'Who caught his blood?' 'I,' said New York,
'On that cruel sidewalk, I caught his blood.'
'Who'll make the coffin?' said Norweigian Wood,
'My wood is good, I'll make the coffin.'
'Who'll make the shroud?' 'We,' said the Beatles,
'With our thread and needles, we'll make the shroud.'
'Who'll dig the grave?' 'I,' said the walrus,
'With my powerful tusks, I'll dig the grave.'
'Who'll be the parson?' 'Father Mackenzie,'
They shout in a frenzy, 'he must be the parson.'
'Who'll be the chief mourner?' 'I,' said Hey Jude,
'He's my flesh and blood. I'll be the chief mourner.'
'Who'll carry the coffin?' 'I,' said the Eggman,
'I am your legman, I'll carry the coffin.'
'Who'll take the ashes?' 'I,' said the widow,
'He was truly my hero. I'll take the ashes.'
'Who'll sing Imagine?' 'Lady Madonna
Our own prima donna, she'll sing Imagine.'
'Who'll toll the bell?' 'I,' said the fool
'Because I can pull, I'll toll the bell.'

And all the free world sent their sighs up to Heaven
When they heard the bell toll for the murdered John Lennon.

Margaret Moriarty

The Game

Testing strength on tested strength
Steel-eyed youth to mellowed man
To cunning craft of age
Oh cruel nagging length

Sweating hell on heaving high
Mercy break to tiring limbs
Impatient youthful gains
That heaving fated sigh

Clinging grip on sweating stick
Heavy booted trampling way
Beginning treads to end
Relentless time so quick

Falling sick on breathless tomb
Encased in hopelessness
Flowering buds upend
The last to leave the womb

John Gray

The Darkest Days Before
The Dawn Of Spring

While walking in the woods today,
Amongst the leaves, brown, crisp and dry,
With little light to lift the sky,
The darkest days before the dawn of spring.
But in the gloom my eyes can see,
Bright green shoots are pushing through,
Promising a fine display of bluebells
And the celandine – with her tiny golden face,
Will bring back beauty to this place
And with these thoughts of new life born,
My heart beings to sing,
On this dark day before the dawn of spring.

Cynthia Shum

My Hometown

York is your ideal holiday destination
It will capture all your fascination
Youngs Hotel became well-known
Where Guy Fawkes, made his home
We've a Minster of which we're proud
Where you can take photos, have a tour round
There's The Shambles with cobbled streets
Quaint shops selling souvenirs, old sweets
We've Bar Walls, round every corner a story
To see York in its blazing glory
Take a cruise, admire the view
York has it all for you.

Dawn May

Untitled

A book to read
A hand to hold
A smile when a loved one draws near
Warmth of a fire, a pet on the mat
Life is worthwhile, no need to chat
Your mind is lost in the wonder of words
There are thin books, fat books
Open the pages the words will enthral
And bring pictures to your mind
Some words make your smile
Some words make you cry
But the meaning of words makes life worthwhile
Time passes by hours turn into days
Days into months, words never fade
From one year old to twenty-one
Words are fun and can be enjoyed by everyone.

J M Waller

The Beautiful Night

The beautiful night,
That seals promises, love, dreams and romance:
The moon in all its glory shines on lovers:
It shines on all creatures and leads us to believe
We shall never see such a sight again.
Perhaps it's because we cannot touch the night,
We cannot fault it, mar it, corrupt it!
The night teaches us about ourselves,
We can hide in the night,
Take off the mask of smiles,
Go naked, laugh, dream, cry, die!
We can give ourselves to the night
And no one will know our fears,
Our hope, for a better tomorrow,
In the long and lonely hours of the beautiful night,
When all the world is sleeping
And we who are not afraid of the night:
Its blackness, its stars, its moon,
Its aloneness, its glorious quietness.
For these are what makes the beauty of the night
A world of its own.
We are lost in the past,
We are lost in the dreams,
We are lost in love.
We are lost in the beautiful world of the night.

Pamela Hanover

Hope

Across the pebbles, across the sand,
be my guide and take my hand.
Give me strength, give me courage,
here is my heart for you to nourish.
A soft breeze to calm my mind,
help me sleep, if you would be so kind.
Soothe my nerves, quiet my brain,
help me see the light again.
Of the future, I am unsure,
hope is guidance not a cure.
Those first steps I must take,
a conscious effort for my sake.
Keep me safe, keep me warm,
banish from me a life forlorn.
All my worries are of little use,
if hope has left me no excuse,
to follow my dreams, follow my thoughts,
a guiding light, you must be caught.
Always there, always caring,
hope is love, hope is sharing.
Hope is a light for you to see,
a wondrous person you can be.
A generous and enlightened soul,
hope will give you, that's your goal.
With hope in your heart and hope in your mind,
a life of peace you will find.

Sara Ladbrook

A Willing Fool

There it hung, beside the entrance door.
Handwritten in black ink –
mounted in an oak frame.
Words of wisdom; 'The Warning'
Interpreted into English they had read . . .

'We, the custodians of the Palazzo Marionette Museum,
By way of polite request;
(Please note we speak not in jest!)
visitors to the museum, not to presume
to look marionettes,
located in the final room,
directly in the eye'.

Was this some sort of joke?
A ploy to lure tourists in?
They were marionettes, puppets;
call them what you will -
things brought to life by means of strings.

Hanging from walls, cocooned in cases -
paraded on Baroque stages.

Made of wood, wax, with porcelain faces.
Some with eyes made of glass,
others hideously painted . . .

With a fusty, musty odour
(moth balls one supposed).
Dressed in a variety of
slowly decaying clothes.

Marionettes . . .
Wooden actors -
meant to re-enact an opera,
tragedy or melodrama.

Artefacts on display.
Puppets – most of which,
in order to preserve them,
having never seen the light of day,
confined as they were
within the walls of this oppressive

villa, this increasingly morbid place.

Marionettes, precious – were they not?
Or were they puppets, toys -
on reflection best forgot?

For it was,
as I stepped into that final room,
that their eyes appeared to me -
or so it felt,
gradually to come alive.
By their eerie look,
they seemed to thrive.
Gaining pleasure in provoking
an irrational fear.

Those faces, with their painted lips and hinged jaws -
not operated by any human hand,
appearing now, almost, as if to sneer.

A willing fool was I,
unable to resist looking them in the eye,
to deny the existence of an evil presence here.

Amongst the marionettes housed,
in the 'bizarre sanctorum' that was
-'The Final Room' -
it was then; I was to know real fear.

Julie Taylor

Grieving Soul Of A Fallen Soldier

It was autumn time, when I first spotted you
I remember this well; the cobwebs and early morning dew.
I was collecting fallen leaves of orange, yellow, red and brown,
When a shadow in the distance stood rooted to the ground.

I saw you standing behind the big oak tree
I was walking to school, you were spying on me.
I saw you sitting on a bench, all alone in the park,
I was on my way home, it was getting quite dark.

It was wintertime, and there was cheer in the air
You were by the chestnut stall, at the annual Christmas fair.
Carol singers sang out, spreading joy to all good men,
But your spirit was low; you walk sadly away from them.

I saw you by the lake; you looked as white as the snow
Snowflakes danced through the air, to the north wind blow.
Sledges glided down the slopes, snowballs flew through the air,
You stood silently watching, no one knew you were there.

It was summertime, and the hottest day of the year
As I lay on the beach reading, I sensed you were near.
The beach was full of families, children laughing, having fun,
You stood there in full uniform, ice-cold in the sun.

I sailed across the ocean, to a land far away
As the boat neared the island, you were there in the bay.
I strolled through the market, buying gifts to take back home,
Near the Statue of Liberty, you sat weeping, and alone.

Springtime, Mother Nature delivered her spectacular show
All around, on the ground, daffodils and tulips begin to grow.
Newborn lambs bleat in wonderment, at the start of something new,
I was on a cruise down the River Thames, and you were on the boat too.

What is that letter held tight in your hand?
The stamp is King George, and addressed to England.
The envelope is sealed; the letter remains unread,
Is it a letter of hope, love and peace, or a letter of dread?

Time is set in distance; we're a million miles apart
Yet sometimes when you're near to me, I think I hear your heart.
I can't smell what you smell like; I can't feel your soft rough skin,
I can't taste the scent of serenity; I can't touch your pain within.

I once witnessed something strange; it appeared one night in a dream
You were standing at the altar's edge, bells tolled, what can this mean?
She glided down the aisle dressed in white from head to toe,
And you were dressed in a bright blue suit, with a bright red dickey bow.

Barely three months later, and your world was torn apart
A ship across the Channel, bound, a cold kiss for your sweetheart.
And as the months passed by, a new arrival entered the world,
She filled the void between you both, bittersweet memories whirled.

Even though I don't know you; for we had never met
I feel a connection between us, you feel the same, I bet.
We have the same blue eyes, and my nose is crooked too,
My hair is black and curly, like yours; do I belong to you?

Angie Dean

Lonely Man

With penetrating gaze
one eyebrow raised
you studied me and my movements.
But more than that
with a personal attention
for the sake of your interest and intention.

And crumpling
I succumbed to your laser beam gaze.
'Where have you been all my life?' you said.
But I mumbled ridiculously instead.

So where do we go from here?
I, a little offbeat,
but conventional in some ways.
And you,
a decade or two older,
but out of character with years -
so much bolder.

So what are years and distances between friends?
For none of that matters in the end.
And the songs will always express
what neither of us dares to confess.

Christine Ann Moore

Forward Poetry
Information

We hope you have enjoyed reading this book - and that you will continue to enjoy it in the coming years.

For free poetry workshops please visit www.forwardpoetry.co.uk. Here you can also join our online writing community 'FP Social' and subscribe to our monthly newsletter.

Alternatively, if you would like to order further copies of this book or any of our other titles, then please give us a call or log onto our website.

Forward Poetry Information
Remus House
Coltsfoot Drive
Peterborough
PE2 9BF

(01733) 890099